D0962137

Praise for *Love Has a Name*

"Loving people is hard! Even on our best days, loving those closest to us can be tough. But the stories Adam tells in *Love Has a Name* show us that love isn't as complicated as we sometimes make it. Because love has a name, and that name isn't Mark or Adam or even yours! That name is Jesus, and when we make love about him, everything else falls into place. Struggling to love? Pick up this book!"

—MARK BATTERSON, *New York Times* bestselling author of *The Circle Maker* and lead pastor of National Community Church

"In *Love Has a Name*, Adam Weber shows us how to love people even when it's painful, tough, and draining. Adam's writing rejuvenates my soul. This book truly ministered to my heart—my longing not just to love Jesus but to love *like* him. Grab this book!"

—RASHAWN COPELAND, founder of I'm So Blessed Daily and author of *Start Where You Are*

"Some of the most powerful moments in our lives are when someone calls us by name. It literally makes our brains fire faster. We feel special. My friend Adam Weber has wrestled this to the ground in *Love Has a Name*. I've watched Adam love people well—he's the right guy to lead this conversation. Adam points us to the one who knows love like no other: *Jesus.*"

—TYLER REAGIN, author of *The Life-Giving Leader* and founder of the Life-Giving Company

"If you find your heart growing callous or if the gospel has become just a series of ideas or propositions, this book will be a tremendous challenge and help. Adam captures the love story of Jesus's life played out in modern-day relationships, and it's beautiful. Thank you for this, Adam. My own heart softened. It needed to."

—CAREY NIEUWHOF, podcaster, speaker, and bestselling author

"My friend Adam Weber is a true catalyst! *Love Has a Name* is a practical book filled with everyday stories about loving others like Jesus did—a mission and purpose all of us should be pursuing."

—BRAD LOMENICK, founder of BLINC and author of *H3 Leadership* and *The Catalyst Leader*

"This book is special. My friend Adam Weber has an amazing way of bringing out deep insights in ways that anyone can understand. This book is full of stories—*normal* stories about normal people like you and me. Each story embodies a unique aspect of love. And each drives us deeper into the sacred embrace of Jesus. You are going to be so blessed!"

—Daniel Fusco, pastor, television and radio host, and author of
Crazy Happy; Upward, Inward, Outward; and *Honestly*

"This book is beautifully personal and powerfully universal. With winsome insight and deep compassion, Adam reveals a God who sees and knows us—yet still unstoppably loves us."

—Katherine and Jay Wolf, survivors, advocates, and
authors of *Suffer Strong* and *Hope Heals*

"In a time of so much outrage, partisan bickering, and 'canceling' people who don't fit our sensibilities, a strong refresher course on love is sorely needed. I can't think of many people more qualified to offer this than my friend Pastor Adam Weber. Every time I encounter Adam, it makes me want to go out and love someone. I trust that will be his impact on you as well."

—Scott Sauls, senior pastor of Christ Presbyterian Church and
author of *Jesus Outside the Lines* and *A Gentle Answer*

"*Love Has a Name* is a love letter to things that are good and true. This is a bright and insightful invitation to see others and ourselves anew, naming what's really been there all along—love."

—Brad Montague, *New York Times* bestselling author and
illustrator of *Becoming Better Grownups*

"Our world is fraught with division, anger, and scorn. We can easily connect through technology yet seem to be drifting apart. In such a scenario, nothing can cut through, redeem, and restore like the love of God. Adam Weber guides us with warmth and humility toward Christ, the source of all love. Read and be inspired to be a vessel of this love in the world."

—Mark Sayers, senior leader of Red Church and
author of *Reappearing Church* and *Strange Days*

"In *Love Has a Name,* Adam Weber destroys the myth that we love based on how we feel. By redefining the way love is demonstrated and acted upon, Adam has given us a field guide for daily love that we will come back to again and again."

—CARLOS WHITTAKER, author of *Enter Wild,* speaker, and storyteller

"Jesus was a master at *seeing* people. It is, in a nutshell, why so many people felt instantly loved by him. Yet in our social media–saturated world, where we engage more with profile pictures than in-person human beings, we are rapidly losing this practice. In these pages Adam models Jesus's ordinary yet world-altering method of love. We need it now more than ever."

—SHARON HODDE MILLER, author of *Nice*

"Scripture tells us that 'God is love.' Jesus incarnated that love, then called his followers to do the same. *Love Has a Name* helps us see what love looks like. This is an inspiring book that will encourage and challenge you."

—ADAM HAMILTON, author of *The Walk*

"Far from theoretical frameworks and philosophical constructs, *Love Has a Name* gets as down to earth as Jesus himself. This book carries something special for our time. And it comes from a voice who knows the subject because he has lived it."

—J. D. WALT, sower-in-chief at Seedbed

"Loving people well doesn't seem like it can change the world. Until it *does.* In *Love Has a Name,* Adam shows us how to do just that. Here's a book filled with everyday stories of loving others like Jesus did, one note of encouragement, neighborhood trash pickup, and bouquet of flowers at a time."

—MIKE FOSTER, bestselling author, speaker, and executive counselor

"Everyone needs a friend like Adam. He's encouraging, kind, selfless, joyful, humble, and patient. As you turn the pages of this book, he'll become your friend and show you how to be a friend to others. This book will help you love other people the way Jesus loves you."

—JON WEECE, lead follower at Southland Christian Church

"Countless books have been written on the subject of love, with authors often resorting to overused slogans and outdated illustrations. Adam Weber's book *Love Has a Name* offers a fresh approach to a timeless topic. This book will inspire and stretch you to be more like Jesus."

—HAL DONALDSON, president of Convoy of Hope

"In *Love Has a Name,* Adam Weber shares gritty real-life lessons about loving others and being loved in return. This love isn't a clichéd three-step recipe to loving better but rather a bold challenge to truly embrace others and show God's love. Through every story Adam continually points us back to Jesus—our ultimate example of true and unconditional love."

—JEREMY DEWEERDT, senior pastor of City First Church

"Adam Weber cares for people deeply. There's almost nothing more important in life than learning how to love people well. There's almost no one better to learn from than my friend Adam, because he loves so well."

—MATT BROWN, evangelist, author of *Truth Plus Love,* and founder of Think Eternity

"Empathy begins when we choose to sit across the table from someone who sees the world differently than we do. I wish every person on social media would read this book before making another comment on someone else's post."

—CHRIS BROWN, speaker, author, and radio and podcast host

"Adam Weber writes with beautiful simplicity that cuts straight to the heart in ways we didn't know we needed. How did the pendulum swing from the tender love of childhood to the cynical callousness of aging? How do we return? We aren't lost, Adam reminds us. Love has a name—Jesus. Life-changing."

—LUKE LEZON, preacher and author of *Your Mess Matters*

"Adam's book comes along at the perfect time. In an age of so much division, he reminds us to stop seeing crowds and start seeing faces. When we see people not as groups but as names, we are drawn together and find God meeting us there. Adam's real-life stories with real-life names call us to return to our greatest commandment—to love God and love others. May we never forget that the others all have names."

—JEFF HENDERSON, author of *Know What You're FOR*

LOVE
HAS A
NAME

LOVE HAS A *Name*

Learning to Love the Different, the Difficult, & Everyone Else

ADAM WEBER

WATERBROOK

Published in the United States by WaterBrook, an imprint of Random House, a division of Penguin Random House LLC.

WATERBROOK® and its deer colophon are registered trademarks of Penguin Random House LLC.

Library of Congress Cataloging-in-Publication Data
Names: Weber, Adam (Pastor), author.
Title: Love has a name : learning to love the different, the difficult, and everyone else / Adam Weber.
Description: First edition. | Colorado Springs, Colorado : WaterBrook, 2020.
Identifiers: LCCN 2020001820 | ISBN 9781601429476 (hardcover) | ISBN 9781601429483 (ebook)
Subjects: LCSH: Love—Religious aspects—Christianity. | Interpersonal relations—Religious aspects—Christianity.
Classification: LCC BV4639 .W357 2020 | DDC 241/.4—dc23
LC record available at https://lccn.loc.gov/2020001820

Printed in the United States of America on acid-free paper

waterbrookmultnomah.com

2 4 6 8 9 7 5 3 1

First Edition

SPECIAL SALES
Most WaterBrook books are available at special quantity discounts when purchased in bulk by corporations, organizations, and special-interest groups. Custom imprinting or excerpting can also be done to fit special needs. For information, please email specialmarketscms@penguinrandomhouse.com.

Hudson, Wilson, Grayson, and Anderson,
thank you for showing me who love is, every single day.
My greatest goal in life is to show you the same.

Love you so much.

—Dad

In honor of my dear friend Jarrid Wilson

1988–2019

You are loved.

Your legacy of love lives on through Juli, Finch, Denham, and every person you crossed paths with.

Contents

Part 3 | **Your Name**

Love is hard.

Loving others used to come so easily.

As kids, we're naturally quick to trust.

Quick to forgive.

Quick to love others.

Strangers almost immediately become friends.

It's why we have to tell kids not to climb into shady-looking vans[1] and accept candy from people they don't know—they trust and love everyone immediately. Kids are more innocent, but they're also more ignorant, and sometimes ignorance truly is bliss. Shorter memories, fewer insecurities—what's not to like about being a kid?

But with each year that passes, it seems like loving people gets a little harder. At some point, our hearts become jaded, cynical, and skeptical.

We become slow to trust.

Slow to forgive.

Slow to love others.

We look for ways to keep our neighbors at a distance. Our relationships now seem to come with scorecards that we use to keep track of how well the other person is loving us. Kids' soccer games and birthday parties are easy to forget, but the mistakes of certain family members never leave our heads.

Friends slowly become strangers.

The older we get, the more difficult love becomes as our relationships (and our lives) get more complicated. If I'm honest, most days I struggle to love anyone. I've never struggled to love people more than I have the past couple of years.

But love is everywhere. Love is something we hear about, post about on social media,[2] and sing about. It's a word we wear on our shirts and even get tattooed on our bodies. For many of us, when the word *love* leaves our lips, it sounds fluffy and beautiful—like sunshine, fairy tales, and unicorns. Who wouldn't want to love others when love is so great? If you're a decent human being with a soul, love is a banner you should carry.

Yet now more than any other time (at least it feels this way to me!), love seems absent from our attitudes, words, and actions. We say we love others, but we really don't. Instead, we're quick to shake our fists at drivers, judge the stranger who looks strange, and trash the person online who thinks differently than we do. We gossip behind the backs of our coworkers and daydream about body-slamming certain family members. Instead of loving people, we hurt, belittle, and overlook them.

Here's the deal, though: Do you remember when your kindergarten teacher wrote the rules of your classroom in the upper right-hand corner of the chalkboard? Can you picture it?

Rule 1: Raise your hand.

Rule 2: Respect your classmates.

And that's all there was! Pretty easy, right? Well, Jesus does the same thing with us when it comes to love.

Rule 1: Love God.

Rule 2: Love others.

Rule 3: There is no Rule 3. That's it. Just do those first two over and over.[3]

According to Jesus, these two "loves" are the two most important things. Simple, right? Maybe. But even with Jesus in our hearts, loving people is much easier said than done. Whether you've been following Jesus for decades or you're still on the fence about God, loving people can be painful, uncomfortable, exhausting, and even grueling at times. Love can hurt.

And Jesus didn't just talk about love *generally*—teaching about love from a stage to an adoring crowd. Instead, Jesus loved people *personally.* He got face to face with people. He didn't just talk about love. He loved specific people.

Sick people. Bad people.

Normal people. Broken people.

Religious people. Judgmental people.

Awkward people. Overlooked people.

Contagious people. Ugly people.

Different people, who were different in every possible way.

Difficult people, who were so incredibly hard to love.

Jesus knew their stories. Who they were. Their names. Their status—or lack thereof. And he loved them anyway.

Jesus shows us that knowing people's stories is the path to fully loving them. The pathway to love always begins with a story. Not *our* stories, but *their* stories. We can't love people if we can't truly see them, and we can't really see and know people without knowing their stories.

That brings us to the journey this book is going to take us on. This isn't a book on "three steps to loving better." This book tells the stories of twenty-seven people (and one school), who opened my heart to loving more fully.

Each of these people has taught me something about loving others. I showed love to some of these people, but in every case I was on the receiving end of love. In many ways, *they* ended up showing *me* what love is all about.

Some of these people are close friends; others are strangers I crossed paths with for only a short time. None of them are famous. None of them have huge platforms or special talents. Maybe you can relate? On the surface, these people might appear to be quite normal, but they're anything but. The truth is, no one is normal. We all have our own unique stories.

The stories here aren't always polished or pretty. In fact, some of them don't have happy endings—or any ending at all yet. But these stories and these people have taught me how to love better, how to love more fully, and how to love as Jesus does, more than any textbook or how-to guide ever could. My hope is that they will do the same for you too.

Before we meet them, though, let's talk about what love is. Actually, let's talk about *who* love is.

You see, love has a name.

Jesus

Love knows you by name.

A few years back, I went to pick up my daughter from a birthday party. She was at one of those gymnastics places where the kids have free rein to jump into foam pits, swing on monkey bars, and do somersaults. To enter the gym area, you have to take off your shoes, so I came in, found a bench, and started to take my shoes off.

As I was untying my laces, I looked over and saw a little kid from the church I pastor.[1] He smiled ear to ear, his eyes wide open, filled with excitement to see me. The kid started tapping his mom's leg to get her attention. At first she didn't look, so he kept tapping. When she finally looked up, he pointed at me and said, "Look, Mom! It's Jesus!"[2] Ha, I have clearly failed as a pastor if a little kid is mistaking me for Jesus!

But he did get one thing right: Jesus is everywhere!

His name. His image. Or at least a *version* of his name and image: Wavy brown hair that would make most ladies (and me) jealous. Deep blue eyes. Always wearing a white bathrobe and sandals like he's ready for a walk on the beach.

Jesus—who appears to be the loving side of a God who's angry at times. His name is the choice word when you stub your toe or hit yet another stoplight when you're already late for work. He's our "homeboy."[3] Our buddy. The dude in the picture frame on your grandma's wall. In art. In songs. Tattoos. On T-shirts. Bumper stickers. Even a piece of toast.[4]

We hear Jesus's name sprinkled throughout conversations between people who haven't been to church in years. Sometimes his name is mentioned at the center of a deep conversation, but more often than not, it's dropped in without much thought.

Even *Newsweek* and the Discovery Channel regularly ask who Jesus is. But who is Jesus, really? The quick answer: A carpenter from a town called Nazareth. The son of Mary and Joseph. That about covers it, right?

Sure, almost.

Oh, and a bunch of us also believe he's God. He was born from his mother, just as we all are born from our mothers, but he was conceived by the Holy Spirit. Know anyone else who was conceived by God? Me neither!

And we believe that he's God with good reason. He gave sight to the blind. Made a dead person come back to life. Walked on water. Fed a few thousand people with a small lunch pail of food. He did and can do all kinds of things.

And he's also perfect, so there's that!

But more than Jesus's ability to turn water into wine or do any other mind-bending miracle, the way he *loves* people is what truly sets him apart. It's the way Jesus loves that makes him so different—at least, so different from me.

He Knows Our Name

There's something special about a person's name. When someone knows and remembers your name, it communicates worth. It helps you feel noticed. Important. Seen. When someone uses your name, it gives you value. Each of us has a longing inside to be known. To be loved. Remembering a name is the first step to knowing someone—to *loving* someone.

Me? I'm terrible at remembering names.[5] I rarely forget a face, but I even struggle to remember my own kids' names sometimes. I use the classic "Hey, man, how's it going?" a lot of times when I can't remember a person's name.[6] Wouldn't it be so much easier if everyone wore a name tag at all times?[7]

Jesus knew people's names, before even meeting them. Not just the names everyone else knew. Not just the names of the public figures verified on Instagram,[8] the religious elite, the well-off. Instead, Jesus used the names of *everyone,* including those society said had no worth—prostitutes, thieves, lepers.

One of my favorite stories ever is about the day Jesus came through the city of Jericho.[9] There was a man there who collected taxes for a living. Basically, he overtaxed and stole money from his own people. To put it nicely: the man wasn't very well liked. And he wasn't just a tax collector, but we're told he was a *chief* tax collector. Not just a jerk, the *chief* jerk!

So, he's not well liked, but he has money. And somehow this man knew about Jesus coming to town, and he wants to see him. Maybe it was the large crowd that intrigued him. Maybe he heard about Jesus's wild teaching and parables. Maybe he knew about the miracles. Maybe he had been told about the blind man who had just been healed outside the city earlier that day.

Whatever the reason was, the man wanted to see Jesus. But there was a problem: he was short. *Very* short. He's a "wee little man."[10] He couldn't see over the crowd to spot Jesus coming into town. But he had an idea. We're told "he ran ahead and climbed a sycamore-fig tree" to see him. Problem solved!

Each time I hear this story, it makes me wonder: What inside this man brought him up that tree? Was something missing in his life? He had made his money; wasn't it enough?

When Jesus reached the man's chosen perch, he looked up at the weirdo among the leaves and said, "Zacchaeus, come down immediately. I must stay at your house today."

Jesus knows his name!

Zacchaeus.

What? He does? Why?

My favorite part is how we're told that "Zacchaeus quickly climbed down and took Jesus to his house in great excitement and joy."

I'm guessing there were times when Zacchaeus didn't want his name to be known—probably by the people whose money he had taken—but he was elated that Jesus knew his name.

The crowd, on the other hand, was ticked. They grumbled and complained that Jesus not only knew Zacchaeus's name but was going to his house, the house of a notorious sinner, to eat. *He's going to go to the house of the jerk who's stealing everyone's money? Shorty's house? How could he?*

If Jesus knows the name of a guy like Zacchaeus, I'm guessing he knows the names of the people in our lives too.

Our ex.

Our friends who hurt us.

Our high-maintenance coworkers.

Our hard-to-love in-laws.

Our frustrating spouses.

The spam callers trying to sell us who-knows-what.

The strange religious people who knock on our front door.

The know-it-alls on Twitter.

Jesus knows their names. Do we? Do we even want to? When we put names with faces, they're no longer just faces in the crowd—they're humans. No matter how much we don't want to admit it, they have value. They have worth. We must remember that God made them, that God loves them, and that we're commanded to love them too.

A name gives a person value. It's hard to believe some people have value, isn't it? But here's a life-changing statement for us: *their lives have the same value as ours.* That's hard to believe sometimes. But it's true. The world might say otherwise and the crowds might shout something different, but Jesus doesn't. He knows each of their names and often walks past crowds of people to go have a meal at the house of the one person we struggle to love the most. He walks past the well-known people to get to the person who appears to be worthless.

Are you starting to understand why the crowds were grumbling that day in Jericho when Jesus went to visit Zacchaeus? I wouldn't have just grumbled; I would have been angry! I would have shouted my outrage because of the one Jesus picked out of the crowd.

But Jesus? He knew *Zacchaeus's* name.

He knows our names too. *My* name.

And yours.

He Knows Our Stories

Jesus not only knows your name and my name and the names of every other human being on the planet (which would make him a great candidate for president of the universe!), but he takes it a step further and knows our *stories* as well.

Jesus knows where we've been and what we've walked through.

Our hardships.

Our losses.

Our regrets.

Our pasts, good and bad.

Our parents.

Our successes.

Our failures.

The things we've never told anyone.

The things we've tried to forget.

He knows it all.

He knows our stories completely—how and why we are the people we are. He knows our stories even better than we do. We see Jesus, on numerous occasions, meeting someone for the first time, and before that person even speaks a word, Jesus makes it clear: he knows their name and their story.

One of these moments is when a guy named Nathanael walked up to Jesus.[11] Nathanael had heard that Jesus is God, but he's fairly doubtful that this word on the street was true. *Jesus the carpenter guy? He's God? Sure, and my name is LeBron,* Nathanael thought.[12]

But Nathanael was curious enough to listen to his friend Philip, who had just met Jesus for the first time. Nathanael followed Philip back to Jesus, but before he even met Jesus, Jesus shouted, "Now here is a genuine son of Israel—a man of complete integrity."

Struggling to find the right words, Nathanael responded, "How do you know about me?" Immediately his defenses fell. Jesus knows him. On a level Nathanael couldn't fully grasp. Jesus knows his story.

Time and time again this happened: A person finds out that Jesus knows his story, and his heart opens up. He immediately feels loved and drawn to Jesus. It's clear Jesus isn't making a snap judgment. He's not labeling him as others have: "sinner," "tax collector," "adulterer." Jesus sees him for who he really is: a person made in his image.

What if one of the best steps to loving the rough-around-the-edges people in our lives starts with knowing their stories? Getting to know them—their names and their past hurts, dreams, passions—so that we can begin to love them? At least for me, this helps. The loud, arrogant coworker is so much easier to love when you find out he didn't have a dad growing up. The person who's known for being easy to sleep with is much harder to judge when you find out she was abused in a previous relationship. The grumpy neighbor is easier to be patient with when you find out he's battling an addiction to alcohol on a day-to-day basis.[13]

Even with the hardest-to-love people, when you start to know their stories, you can't help but have compassion, kindness, and love begin to well up within you. Instead of snapping back, you give them the benefit of the doubt. Instead of gossiping, you pray for them. Instead of avoiding them, you invite them in. Even when it's really hard to see, you begin to notice bits and pieces of the good and the image of God inside of them.

And when you do, even the hardest-hearted person begins to open up her soul and let her defenses drop. We find ourselves changing, too, as loving others leads us into a better life. Love is something we're all longing for.

Grace and Truth

Jesus knows our names and stories, and he offers us grace and truth.

Life and relationships are messy, and so is love. Often when we talk about love, we think about a sappy movie or Taylor Swift's latest song. But love is anything but light and fluffy.

True love isn't easy. True love is hard. At times, it involves grace. Forgiving someone. Seeing the best in people who don't have much good in them. And other times, it involves speaking the truth.

"I love you enough to say something you don't want to hear."

"No, this is not okay."

"I love you, but we need some boundaries."

"I love you enough to say you need help, and I'm willing to walk alongside you."

Love is a lot like a coin. It has two sides—grace and truth. When you flip it, it can land on heads or tails, but you need both sides in order to flip it.

Most of our coins are weighted, though. For some of us, our coins always land on grace, while others always land on truth. When we lean toward grace, everyone knows they can push us around. We become the people everyone seeks out when they want to feel better about themselves. There are certain things we should say and need to say, but we never do.

The rest of us are truth tellers. We speak our minds too often. We live by the law and pretty much see it as our duty to call people out when they cross the line. We're like hall monitors, except not for the hallways of an elementary school but for life.

Thankfully, Jesus is both grace *and* truth! And because he's both, he's not a pushover or a hall monitor. He's someone so different and otherworldly that we're drawn to him.

John, a guy who knew Jesus personally, once said Jesus was "full of grace and truth."[14] John meant that Jesus has complete grace and complete truth. Not fifty-fifty, but one hundred percent grace and one hundred percent truth. Jesus is both!

Everyone wanted to be as close to Jesus as they could get. Drawn to his loving grace, they knew they were accepted and not condemned. Drawn to his loving truth, they wanted to know his ways and the path that led to life, even if it contradicted the ways they were living.

Get this: when our words, actions, and lives have both grace and truth, people will be irresistibly drawn to God's love flowing and spilling out of our lives. People won't be drawn to us but to Jesus in us.

One Last Thing

There's one last thing to know before we jump into the rest of the book, and it's important: Jesus doesn't *just* love people.

You and I *attempt* to love people. Jesus does more than that.

John hung out, walked around, and lived with Jesus, and he also said something shocking. It may not be shocking to you, particularly if you grew up in the church, but during the time Jesus lived, it would have been crazy talk. During Jesus's time, God was someone you were supposed to fear. His holiness was emphasized. God had all kinds of commandments and laws you needed to make sure you followed. Because it was impossible to follow all the laws, each year you had to bring an animal to the temple so it could be killed, and you would then be forgiven of all the ways you'd screwed up in the last year.[15]

Again, back in Jesus's day, you would have clearly known that God is just and holy and not at all like you. But John said something crazy. Wait for it . . .

"God is love."[16]

Yep, God is love. Yes, he is holy, but he is also love.

Don't miss it: He doesn't just love. Love isn't just something he does. It's *who* he is!

What does that mean? How does that look? Thankfully, John responds and tells us more: "I'm so glad you asked. This is how we know what real love is—Jesus gave up his life for us."[17]

Don't understand what love looks like? Don't truly understand God's love and how to love others? Thankfully, love has a name!

• • •

Love has a name: *Jesus.*

Jesus! He is who love is.

And Jesus says that loving God is the most important thing.

Hear this: people will know our love for God by the way we *love others.*

Not by our church attendance. Not by how many Bible verses we have memorized. Not by all the good religious things we do. Not even by our theology.

All of these things are important and good. But according to John,

> If anyone says, I love God, and hates a brother or sister, he is a liar, because the person who doesn't love a brother or sister who can be seen can't love God, who can't be seen. This commandment we have from him: Those who claim to love God ought to love their brother and sister also.[18]

People will know our love for God by *the way we love* them and others and ourselves. That's it. Plain and simple.[19] But it's not so simple at all. Loving people sounds easy until we get to the "loving people" part.

• • •

Now, we're barely scratching the surface here, but thankfully Jesus is going to be with us throughout this book. In each chapter, we'll learn a bit about how to love others by the way Jesus loved specific people—by getting to know their names, their stories, and then meeting them with his grace and truth. (Oh, and don't forget to read all the field notes in the back!)[20]

This book is about looking to Jesus (not me) and learning how to love based on the way he loves others. I'm clearly a work in progress in this area, so let's learn together.

I can't wait to introduce you to some of the people who have helped me learn love's name.

PART 1

Some People Who Have Loved Me

God does not love some ideal person,
but rather human beings just as we are.

—Dietrich Bonhoeffer

2

Jake

Love pursues the unpopular.

From the first day I met Jake in my kindergarten classroom, I knew he was cool.

Unlike any of the other sticky-fingered six-year-old kids in my class, Jake had railroad tracks sharply buzzed into the sides of his hair.

He was hip. Later, he'd be the first in my fifth-grade class to wear Girbaud jeans.[1]

We always had so much fun together. Jake had the *coolest* tree fort in his backyard. Between that and a sweet arsenal of toy guns, our imaginary battles were epic. When we got tired of that, his football gear came out—complete with pads, jerseys, and real helmets. He would turn into Joe Montana, and I would be Ickey Woods.[2]

Jake was one of the most popular kids in my grade. Everyone wanted to be his friend. More than being popular, though, Jake was my friend—such a great friend that I named a chicken after him.[3] Somehow our moms became friends too, so we got to see each other all the time. In school and out of it, we were always together.[4] I had other friends, but Jake was my *best* friend.

We'd hang out with a group of friends, but with each year that passed, the other kids would try harder to fit in, and so would I. As Jake and the others got cooler, somehow I got nerdier.

Just so you can picture me, I was the first kid in my class to get glasses.[5] I wasn't the best at sports. To top it off, I had strange curly hair and pimples. (Oh, how I dream of that curly hair now!)[6]

All this to say: I was the opposite of popular, which made me an easy target. I was picked on plenty. But who was always there? Jake. He didn't care if I was chosen last at recess football. He didn't seem to gauge whether or not it was cool to be around me. Each year I got invited to his awesome birthday parties, but more than that, I was his first choice when he got to invite a friend over to his house. Other friendships came and went, but Jake was always there, excited to hang out with me. We'd talk about who knows what. When I was excited, I couldn't wait to tell him why. When I felt foolish, I knew he would listen. I could tell him anything.

Jake was a consistent friend, each and every day. It didn't matter where we were. It didn't matter whom we were with. Love is consistent like that.

The memory of Jake's continual presence has stayed with me over the years. He made me feel like I mattered. For any elementary kid trying to find himself, there's so much that's uncertain. Jake's friendship was something I never had to question.

One specific memory with Jake that I'll never forget happened during a field-trip bus ride.[7] One of the girls in my class kept calling me "four eyes." I always did my best to avoid being the center of attention, but whenever someone called me out, humor was my best defense.

That day, I tried to be funny and laugh off the "four eyes" comments, even though the words hurt. I mean, I didn't really like my glasses either! I secretly hated them. But this time, humor didn't work to get the girl off my case, and she continued to make fun of me.

Jake saw what was going on and switched seats so he could sit next to me. In his kind, friendly way, he simply said to the girl, "Well, that's not very nice." He didn't lash out or make her feel embarrassed, yet he made it clear that he wanted her to leave me alone. And she did.

I sat back in my seat, relieved. I took a deep breath. It meant the world to me that Jake not only would sit by me but would also defend me.

After sixth grade, my family moved to a new town eighty miles away.[8] Jake and I kept in contact and remained friends, getting together with each other's families every so often, but it was different with eighty miles between us.

In college, by a random twist of fate, we ended up at the same school, in the same dorm, on the same floor during our freshman year.[9] By then, Jake and I were headed in different directions in life—not better or worse, just different. But what hadn't changed? How endlessly thankful I was for Jake's friendship in elementary school. That year (and many times since), I was able to pull Jake aside and tell him thank you.[10] It honestly felt kind of strange to say thank you so many years later. Yet I've found it's never too late to thank people for what they've done.[11]

Starting way back in kindergarten, Jake taught me that love stands by someone when no one else will. It means being there even when it doesn't make you popular, staying when others ridicule you. Jake taught me about loyalty. About love. About how to make someone feel important. About loving another person even if it means you'll be doing it alone. About how to sit next to the person who has four eyes and defend him.

It's easy to stand by someone when you have nothing to lose. Anyone can do that.

But what about when it isn't popular? It's just you. And that person.

I thank God for Jake "the Snake" Schlueter.

• • •

I've already mentioned tax collectors (remember Zacchaeus?), yet Jesus talked about them often and come April 15 of every year we have to deal with them as well,[12] so I think it's all right that I talk about them a time or two myself. I don't think anyone loves taxes, and in Jesus's day, tax collectors were known for overcharging their people. They were super rich because they had screwed everyone else over. To put it simply, tax collectors were not part of the popular crowd.

So, these tax collectors were treated as outcasts, labeled as outrageous sinners. Often they appear as a group of nameless people Jesus interacted with—sitting and eating, listening and talking. But every so often, we're told one of their names. One specific tax collector we meet through Jesus is a guy named Levi.

One day Levi was sitting at his usual spot, his tax collector booth near a main road, when Jesus approached him.[13] "Follow me," Jesus said. (Jesus's invitation can also translate to "join me" or "accompany me.")

If you grew up hearing this story a bunch of times, then this invitation from Jesus might seem obvious. *Of course, Jesus invites us to follow him! That's what Jesus does.* But if you haven't heard this story before—or better yet, if you've ever felt like an outsider, an outcast, uncool, or unlovable—then an invitation of any kind is a big deal! There are few things better than being invited. And few things better than another person, especially a popular guy like Jesus, inviting you to join him.

Jesus *invited* Levi! Jesus pursued him. And what did Levi do? He felt so loved by Jesus that he asked Jesus to come to his house. He was going to throw a party. And Jesus said, "Yes. I'm in." Jesus wasn't afraid to be seen with Levi, and he also wasn't afraid to be seen at Levi's house, hanging out at Levi's party.

Where are the popular kids? Where are the people who followed all the rules and lived seemingly perfect lives? We're not really sure. They're nowhere to be seen. Maybe they were at their own exclusive party for the in-crowd, but Jesus decided that wasn't the place for him. He'd rather hang with the outsiders, the unpopular. Jesus would rather be a friend of sinners than of the people who think they have it all figured out. He chose Levi. And he chooses you and me.

And before we start believing that Jesus was applauded by everyone for befriending Levi, get this: because of his friendship with Levi, Jesus himself was ridiculed and bullied.

"Why does he eat with such scum?" people asked. But Jesus didn't walk away. He didn't hide. Instead, he stood by Levi when no one else would. He was a friend when no one else was there. Instead of chasing popularity, Jesus pursues the unpopular.

• • •

At our lowest points in life, we often find out who our true friends are. You'll find out who's simply a fan of your life and who's a friend. Fans come and go. Fans are fickle. Fans leave when it's not convenient for them. But friends remain. And a lot of the time, they're the people we least expect to stay.

Early on for me, that friend was Jake. He was there when no one else was, showing me at a young age what a true friend looked like. I have him to thank for getting me through elementary school. Those first years of school (not to mention, the rest of my life) would have looked so very different if it wasn't for Jake and his amazing railroad-track haircut.

For Levi, that friend was Jesus. Jesus invited Levi to be part of what he was doing, and in turn Levi invited Jesus into his house and ultimately his life.

Jesus didn't look down on Levi when everyone else did, just like Jake didn't make fun of me and my curly hair and brown glasses. But loving when it's unpopular is more than just not being mean. Jesus challenges us to do more. It's not enough to simply not be part of the problem. Jesus asks us to go further. He asks us to invite people in—into our friend groups, into our home, into our lives.

Who is it that you need to invite in?

One of your coworkers?

A neighbor?

A family member?

The weird person in your class?

Someone who doesn't really have anyone else?

Sadly, when it comes to inviting people into our lives, we as adults can often be worse than middle-schoolers at lunchtime. We have our cliques and groups, our preconceived notions. Like the kid who's afraid that sitting with the nerd will make him a nerd, we don't reach out because we're afraid of what it might say about us, afraid of what we might lose.

Think of that person in your life who has messed up. Maybe lost her job. Had an affair. Went to rehab. Once part of the popular clique, she's now fallen from grace and landed on the outside.

Invite that person back in! Jesus stood with people; he invited them in. When others distance themselves, Jesus gets closer. Closer to the hurting person. Closer to the person who screwed up. Closer to the outcast.

Are you quick to run and hide when it's not popular to stay? Quick to hope someone else reaches out so it doesn't have to be your reputation on the line? Or are you standing firm with someone, no matter what other people say? Are you inviting people in, not closing them off? Sadly, Christians are often the worst at this. Not all, but some.

Just imagine what it would look like if we actually lived this out. What if Christians were known as people who got closer? If the church was known for caring about people instead of walking away from them?

Hurting people wouldn't be left alone. People who made mistakes would know they weren't defined by those mistakes. At their lowest moments, they would be surrounded by love. In our darkest days, others (including ourselves) would experience the love of Jesus as never before.

Want to love like Jesus does? Pursue the unpopular rather than pursuing popularity. Seek out the unpopular kids (or grown adults).

Associate with the classmate or coworker whom others keep distant. When someone screws up, be the person who gets closer to that person as others are walking away.

It's amazing how much power there is in an invitation. Jesus was the best at making people feel like they belonged. Making the person who was different feel known. Including the person who felt left out.

Just to warn you, what happened to Jesus when he hung out with Levi will most likely happen to us too. When we begin to pursue the unpopular, others will distance themselves from us. People will judge and criticize us. Some will walk away from us.

But who really cares? I mean, *really*. Be like Jesus anyway! Think of Jesus going to Levi's house. Think of Jake hanging out with the unpopular kid, me. Think of those who have stood by you when no one else did.

And choose to love like that.

3

Joy

Love multiplies for others.

When I was growing up, my dad was an electrician. A few years after he graduated high school, he started an electrical business, and it quickly grew.[1] In our small town, his business became a fairly big deal. My dad worked for years to get where he was financially, with a beautiful home on acreage on the edge of town, cash-purchased family vehicles, and a hobby farm with every random animal under the sun. If my dad could dream up an idea, we were able to do it. Life really couldn't have been much better.

That is, until the car accident. One night, my parents were going to get pizza, and someone pulled out in front of them. Dad was completely okay except for his right knee. In the wreck his leg had hit the dash, and his knee paid the price. One total knee-reconstruction surgery later, my dad lost his ability to kneel, crawl, and climb ladders, making it next to impossible for him to be an electrician.

My dad ended up selling his electrical business and purchasing a hardware store, moving our family an hour away to Clark, South Dakota, the town where I would live until I left for college.[2] Buying the store was a good business decision at the time. But every year after my parents bought the store, the area flooded, hurting the local farmers financially, which in turn hurt my parents' hardware store. With each year that passed, my parents sank further into debt.

Soon it became clear that my parents wouldn't be able to pay back the loan they had taken out from the bank to finance the store. Like my dad trying to climb a ladder with his busted knee, it was impossible to climb out of the debt they found themselves in. Yet my dad had made a promise to the bank he intended to keep.

It was our family pastor who finally convinced my dad that filing for bankruptcy was the right thing to do, even if it felt wrong. It was one of the hardest days of my dad's life. Even though the letters were really small, it crushed my dad that his name and the word *bankruptcy* would show up together in our town's newspaper.

To make matters worse, we couldn't stay in the home we were living in. Would we live in an apartment? Would we rent a place? That's when Joy stepped in. A single woman in her fifties with no kids, Joy had heard about my parents' situation through a mutual friend. Joy and another woman who owned a realty company wanted to help us buy a home.[3]

That seemed like a nice thought to my parents, but they knew they would never be able to get a loan from the bank. After hearing more of my parents' story, though, Joy said she and her business partner would loan my family the money themselves. All of it. Even though my parents were thrilled with the offer, they couldn't imagine it coming without a catch, especially since Joy barely knew them. But Joy said there was no catch; she simply wanted to help, and so she did.

Looking back, Joy was the hand of God working in my family's life. Not only did she make it possible for us to have a home, but in many ways she rescued my dad from the feeling of being a failure, helping him take the first steps toward dignity again.

The hardware store may have been a bad move financially, but remember my dad's leg that didn't work? Well, each day in the store, my dad would walk miles back and forth helping customers. Doing all that walking on the store's perfectly flat floors allowed my dad's leg to safely heal, and slowly but surely he was able to fully use his leg again. A miracle! This meant he could go back to being an electrician, the work he loved, once again.

Even in our hard seasons of life, God is up to good.

Who was one of my dad's first customers when he started doing electrical work again? Joy. She had him wire a house she was building for someone else. Soon after, she hired my dad again. And again and again.

During a couple of summers while I was in college, I ended up indirectly working for Joy myself, wiring houses with my dad. On one of those summer days, Joy called up my dad and asked us to come hear about a dream she had. We drove outside of town a few miles and met Joy, who walked us through a wide-open pasture with rolling hills and tall grass as far as the eye could see. Her dream was to build a retreat center and a large camp on the land. Joy loved horses, and for years she'd worked with them to help rehabilitate kids with special needs and wounded vets.

But Joy wanted to do more. As she spoke about the small western town she would build—with a Main Street, vintage western buildings, and everything—I honestly thought she might be losing it. At best it was a dream that would remain just that, a dream.

Years passed and I never thought anything more of Joy's dream, until one day, years later, when I was driving and saw a sign for "Joy Ranch." It wasn't until the fifth or sixth time I saw the large sign that I began to realize it was the same Joy I knew.

Her dream had become a reality, bigger and nicer than the vision she had first explained to me and my dad. And now, each year, *hundreds* of adults and kids come to visit Joy Ranch. There are retreats for kids who have been sexually abused, gatherings for families with disabilities, getaways for wounded vets, church camps, business retreats, family reunions.

You name it, Joy Ranch hosts it.[4]

About a year ago, Joy reached out to my dad and said she wanted to host a staff retreat for Embrace (the church where I'm a pastor). All thirty or so of us. Free of charge. She said, "We just want you to come and enjoy yourselves." And we did just that. An hour or so after we arrived, Joy quietly stopped by to say hello. She wanted to make sure we had everything we needed. When Joy left us, most of the staff had no idea who she even was. Joy likes it that way.

Generosity isn't something just Joy does, though. Her generosity has multiplied because it has inspired others to give. Joy Ranch is not just the result of what she's given—it's the result of what so many others have given as well. It's a vision so remarkable that it's contagious.

When I first started following Jesus, I can remember being moved by Joy's generosity to my family. After seeing my parents go through their bankruptcy, as a sophomore in high school, I decided I would never get to that place financially. I'd make as much money as I could, and I'd keep it. I'd make more money so I could keep more money. Yet there Joy was, giving her hard-earned money away.

A seed of generosity was planted in me. That seed would take root and slowly grow throughout my adult life. Joy's generosity to my family made me want to be generous toward others.[5] I know there are countless people like my parents who have been touched by Joy's love and led to take what they have and place it in God's hands.

Love multiplies for the good of others.

. . .

Joy's story reminds me of a person Jesus met. Someone who's often overlooked in a book full of heroes, prophets, and other big names.

Who? A young boy—in some translations he's called a "young boy" or "lad."[6] (I tried calling one of my sons "young lad" once, and he looked at me like I was crazy. I told him it was biblical!) We know nothing about this lad himself—no descriptions or details are shared. All we know is what he has in his hands: five loaves of bread and two fish. This young boy is the perfect example of someone being used by God. How? He simply offered what he had. He placed what he had in the hands of Jesus.

Jesus had started teaching and healing people, and as a result crowds were following him around. Big crowds. Who wouldn't want to meet a guy who could give sight to the blind and make a person with bad legs walk? I can remember wanting to stay up late to watch the magician David Copperfield do cool things on TV,[7] but what Jesus was doing was even greater.

After one day of teaching, the crowd of people hanging around Jesus was getting hungry. All five thousand of them, plus women and children. Miracles are great, but when the hangry sets in, it doesn't take long for a quiet crowd to turn into a menacing mob.[8]

Those closest to Jesus said they needed to tell the people to leave and go find food, but Jesus had another idea. "I'll feed them," he told his crew. "What do we have to work with?" Jesus's crew filled him in: "All we have is a young boy with the five loaves of bread and two fish he packed for lunch." Clearly not enough, right?

But they went up to the boy anyway, taking what he had and placing it in the hands of Jesus. What happens next is what we're still talking about thousands of years later: Jesus took the boy's generosity and he *multiplied* it, feeding five thousand–plus people that day. And this wasn't just a little snack. Nope—"they all ate as much as they wanted."

Jesus kept multiplying, though. After everyone was full, the disciples gathered twelve baskets of leftovers. Twelve! God's math doesn't make sense.[9]

5 + 2 = 5,000 + 12 baskets left over. That's . . . impossible.

All this because of the generosity of one young boy: the lad.

All that because of the generosity of one person: Joy.

• • •

Joy's not very tall. She's the opposite of flashy or fancy. In a crowd or even a small group of people, she's easily overlooked—unseen in the best way possible. At the end of her life, I believe many people will speak of witnessing God and his great love through Joy's actions. Many won't remember her name, but just like the young lad, they'll remember what she held in her hands and gave away. Maybe it'll be a story remembered by thousands. In my eyes, that's the best legacy a person can leave.

I can't remember her name, but have you heard about the miracle God performed through her?

When you take what you have—money, time, love—and you put it in the hands of God, it can't help but multiply.

Struggling to love? Feel like you don't have much? Start giving away what you do have. Be generous and put it in God's hands. Give away your time. Give away your money. Give away your connections. Give away your life.

When you gather bread and hold on to it, the bread gets moldy after a while. Just ask the Israelites what happened when they tried to do that with the bread God gave them.[10] The same happens when you hoard what you have. It begins to mold and stink up your life.

Ever met someone who holds on to all his money, his time, his possessions? His life begins to stink pretty fast. Arrogance sets in. He becomes defensive of everything and obsessed with the idea that everyone is just out for his money, which might be true at times. A blessing becomes a curse.[11] But when you start giving things away, somehow, someway, things will begin to multiply—or maybe you'll just realize that you already had plenty to start with. Plenty for not just yourself but also others. All of a sudden, love will start flowing into every other part of your life.

• • •

I think inside of all of us, we want to be generous, but we don't know where to start. We want to do good. We want to be a blessing. But how?

Have some extra cash this month? Buy dinner for a young family when you're out to eat.

Not sure what to do with your extra time on Tuesday nights? Mow the lawn for your neighbors (maybe ask first!). Or shovel their snow. Offer to babysit for a couple you know would love a date night. Find a car for someone who needs one to get to work. Go to a nursing home and ask if there's someone who needs a visitor. Put money in your pocket this week and give it away. Bake cookies for your neighbors. Start giving regularly to your church. Give an outrageously large tip to the person who cleans your room next time you're at a hotel. Get flowers for someone going through a trial. Volunteer your skills at a school or a nonprofit in town.[12]

See a specific need and fill it. Figure out what you've been generously given—no matter how small—and start giving it away.

We *all* have something to contribute. Maybe it's money. Maybe it's time. Maybe it's extra zucchini from the garden (those things take over!). The point is that you have more than you need, so give to someone who doesn't have enough.

Why give away what you've worked so hard to have in the first place? Because all that we have was never ours in the first place. Everything was given to us by someone else in the past and by God.

One of the greatest moments in our lives is the moment when we discover that the words of Jesus are true: it's greater to give than it is to receive.[13] This is true of love. It's also true of money. We are most like Jesus when we are giving.

When we realize that everything we have is never truly ours, it becomes easy to be generous. It's like giving away someone else's riches. The more you give, the easier it will become. Waiting for someone to ask you to give? I just did![14]

• • •

Recently, I asked Joy about her life and the generosity that flows throughout every part of what she does. She shared that at first giving was hard for her.

"It goes against the way we're wired," she said. "We've earned it. I've earned it, so it should be mine to keep, right? But after you start giving, it becomes contagious. It becomes a way of living and I can't imagine anything different. I call it the road to happiness."

I want to be on that road to happiness, don't you?

I can't imagine a world without a person like Joy in it—a person who's modeled her life after a young lad who gave all he had and watched Jesus multiply it. Even though that kind of generosity may seem crazy or impossible for us, it's really not. Jesus would say it should be the norm. Start with something small. Start by simply giving what you already have; place it in God's hands, and watch him work. When you do, I know that you, too, will begin to walk the road to happiness that Joy so often talks about.

Love multiplies for the good of others.

4

Antonio

Love adores extravagantly.

I first met Antonio while I was preaching. Yep, it was a Sunday and I was onstage when I first "met" him. I was sharing about some of the hard things that people experience in life, the trials life brings where you wonder if you'll make it through:

Losing a job.

A miscarriage.

A cancer diagnosis.

Divorce.

As I began to list off hardships, I heard something in the crowd. Someone . . . laughing? Now, I've learned to preach through pretty much anything: kids screaming, people in the front row getting up to use the bathroom, old guys snoring (it's always the guys), even giant flies dive-bombing my notes,[1] but I have to admit, I paused for a second.

Who laughs at divorce or losing a child?

Maybe the person had heard me wrong and thought it was a joke or had gotten a funny text message from a friend.[2] When the burst of laughter stopped, I continued with my message.

The following week, I was again talking about something heavy and heard laughter in the middle of it. *What is going on?*

After the service, I mentioned the ill-timed laughing to our campus pastor, asking if I'd missed something. He just smiled and said, "Let me introduce you to Antonio."

We went on a brief walk through the after-service crowd. He led me over to a short African American guy wearing fingerless gloves, holding a cup of coffee with both hands. Antonio!

The minute he saw me walking toward him, he started shaking, giddy with excitement. I was tempted to turn around. Like, was the Biebs behind me or something?[3] Could this guy—whom I'd never met—be this excited to see me?

"Hi, my name's Adam," I said.

"H-i-i-i-i," he responded sheepishly.

"What's your name?"

He nervously responded, "An-to-ni-o."

"How are you doing?"

"G-o-o-o-d."

"Do you come to church here often?"

"Yeah-h-h-h."

The more we talked, the more excited Antonio got, responding to all my questions with drawn-out, one-word answers. This short interaction with Antonio may not seem like a big deal to you, but it meant so much to me. I felt so *loved*. He made me feel special. He made me feel like the most important person in the room. In our two-minute conversation, Antonio loved me extravagantly.

The word *adore* means "to cherish, to treasure." Antonio talked with me like he'd found a treasure. I had his full attention. He wasn't distracted. He was truly ecstatic to talk with me. Antonio listened to every word I spoke, and his excitement to meet me was visible.

At a young age, Antonio had a seizure that resulted in severe brain damage. Even though he's now twenty-one years old, he has the understanding of a ten-year-old. Yeah, sometimes he laughs during a worship service when I'm talking about something that isn't funny, such as divorce, but that's part of what makes him unique. From time to time, we've had people mention that Antonio was distracting them from connecting to the message and ask if he could be quieter.

Many people tend to avoid people like Antonio since they don't understand them. Antonio wears a permanent smile that's a bit hard to read if you've never met him. Is he being sincere? That and the way his hands shake make him different. Many people feel awkward when they attempt to engage him in conversation, since he offers only one-word responses. But even though Antonio is an awkward, simple guy, there's another thing that sets him apart: when you're with him, you can't help but feel totally and completely *loved*. In my experience with human beings, that's hard to find.

After meeting Antonio that first week, each time he saw me in the entryway on a Sunday, he would start smiling and shaking uncontrollably. Holding his cup of coffee in both hands like his life depended on it, he would come up to me and say hi, even if I was mid-conversation with someone else. He'd stand close by, smiling, even if I was praying for someone.

Each Sunday I began to look forward to these moments with Antonio. Far from feelings of awkwardness, I found myself hoping we would cross paths.

One day while I was driving around town, I saw Antonio on an outing with some friends from his group home. I rolled down my window. "Hey, Antonio!" I shouted. I hadn't thought it through very well, because when Antonio heard his name, he froze, smiling and shaking. In the middle of a crosswalk. In the middle of a road with lots of traffic. He started looking for the voice. Once he realized it was me, he began waving enthusiastically in my direction. I waved back—but then encouraged him to keep walking so he didn't get hit by a car. "Antonio, keep walking! Keep going!" As I drove away, I couldn't stop smiling. It was the highlight of my day!

Antonio is one of my favorite people on the planet. I'm better because of him. Just thinking about him makes me smile. He's a joy spreader! Our church is better because of him. Oftentimes, I think Antonio is Jesus in our midst. Reminding us not to take ourselves too seriously. Reminding us who and what is really important. The world is better because of him.

Antonio has taught me that love adores extravagantly.

• • •

On one occasion, Jesus was eating with a religious leader in the community, a Pharisee named Simon. As Jesus and his religious leader friend sat down for dinner, a "certain immoral woman" approached Jesus.[4] This lady wasn't just any sinner but was a publicly known sinner, most likely a prostitute, named Mary.[5] To say that Mary was disrupting the meal and the religious leader's time with Jesus would have been the understatement of the year.

We're told that the woman knelt down beside Jesus and began to pour out "a beautiful alabaster jar filled with expensive perfume." This jar of perfume would have been worth an entire year's salary for a working man at this time, not to mention what it would have been worth to a woman like Mary who made a living as a prostitute. By pouring the perfume on Jesus's feet, Mary is literally taking all she has and pouring it all out on Jesus.

Mary then undoes her hair and begins to dry the perfume off of Jesus's feet. This may seem kind of strange to us, but it was a serious no-no at the time. Women were required to wear their hair up; in fact, wearing it down in public marked a woman as having loose morals. Scandalous. Instead of calculating what would be seen as correct or proper, all Mary considers in the moment is her love for Jesus. Even though she is a publicly known sinner, she wants to be near him. She lavishes Jesus with her love. She shows Jesus a love that adores extravagantly.

Don't miss it: in this moment, Mary and Antonio are so much alike. Disregarding what others might think. Going beyond the norms of "polite society" to love in a way that is extravagant. Sure, others might think it's awkward, disruptive, or downright weird, but what Mary did here for Jesus and what Antonio does for me every time he sees me on a Sunday (or in the middle of a crosswalk!) are prime examples of a love that adores extravagantly, no matter what others might think.

To Mary, Jesus was the single most important person in the room, the only she considered in that moment. She was focused solely on him. On the other hand, I can almost feel the religious leader arrogantly staring at her, hoping she'll leave so he can have Jesus's undivided attention. *What is this woman, this prostitute, doing interrupting our time? We have things to talk about here! And I'm much more important than the trash of a person she is.*

Others would have thought she was crazy (kind of like Antonio during my messages), but Jesus simply felt loved—loved so well.

Now, we could end things here, but what's even more amazing than the love Mary showed Jesus is the love Jesus showed her.

Jesus knew everything about Mary from the moment she walked in the door. He knew the depth of her sin, the depth of her story, her past, and all the men she'd been with, better than anyone—and better even than she did. And even though Jesus was eating with this super-religious person most looked up to, whom was Jesus drawn to? Whom did he treat like a VIP? To whom did he give his undivided attention?

Mary.

Jesus didn't see Mary as a distraction but as the focal point.

He sees people like Mary and Antonio. People whom others might see as interruptions. Unnecessary. Out of place. Beneath others. And he treats each person like he or she is the most important person in the room.

With Mary, instead of doing what was correct and proper, Jesus did what was unexpected and taboo. Instead of pushing her away, he allowed her to come near. Instead of condemning her, Jesus associated with her. In Jesus's eyes, Mary wasn't defined by what she had or hadn't done. Instead, she was now defined by Jesus and the extravagant love he had for her.

Extravagant love sets up a holy opportunity for extravagant love in return. It almost demands it! This is part of its power.

Mary would go on to become one of the most well-known friends of Jesus and, without question, one of the most well-known women in all of history. In fact, the Bible says that wherever Jesus is talked about around the world, people will mention Mary and her generous act.[6] The Bible literally says that Mary is famous. Because she adored Jesus extravagantly.

• • •

What if people like Antonio (and Mary) are meant to be reminders of Jesus's extravagant love for and adoration of us? Yes, during a church service but also throughout our week. I've found that often-times the "distractions" in our lives, whether people or events, are the things Jesus wants us to see, hear, and pay attention to the most.[7] On Sundays, instead of being a distraction from the message, what if Antonio is the "message" God wants us to hear?

Antonio has so much to give in our cell phone–addicted society. He's not glued to his screen. He doesn't judge me by my likes or witty online posts. He loves me well simply by making me his central focus in that first moment at church—and a whole lot of moments after that. Because we often love others only if they have something significant to offer us in return, Antonio's extravagant love is refreshing. It's given with no strings attached.

I don't need to earn his attention; he freely gives it. I don't need to try to impress him or act like someone I'm not; he loves me for the person I am. Antonio makes me feel I have worth.

That I matter. That I am loved.

Because I do. And I am.

Even when I don't feel like it's true.

The truth is, there's something special inside each of us. God says we are made in his image.[8] We may not see it, but we are. Humans are different from any other living thing on earth. We, fearfully and wonderfully made, resemble God.[9] Each of us has a gift to offer humanity. Each of us is important to someone. Even if we're important to no one else, each of us is important to God. There is something within us that is divine, that points to our heavenly Creator. God looks at us and says that we are good.

Jesus loves extravagantly. Antonio does the same. I want to learn to love others that way.

• • •

Extravagant love without conditions seems ridiculous at first. It's outside our comfort zone. It's hard. It's a lot of work. Extravagant love takes up time we don't really have to give. Perhaps you're thinking, *Maybe I'll extend love if someone loves me extravagantly first.* But try it once and you'll never be able to go back to loving people any other way. Stepping outside your comfort zone to make someone feel special—there's something about it that's contagious. Loving extravagantly turns the focus from self to someone else, something both Antonio and Mary can teach us.

It doesn't take a huge party or something expensive or elaborate either. Each person, deep inside, simply wants to know: *Will you love me? Will you notice me?* Antonio answers my unspoken question with a resounding *yes,* treating me like his favorite person each time he spots me. In turn, I want to love other people in that same extravagant way.

Antonio may be different than most people, but he's different in a good way! He has so much to teach us about what love should look like.

So, who are the people in your life that you can love extravagantly?

The unseen VIPs who'd appreciate feeling known and loved.

An elementary-school kid who needs a mentor in his life.

The new coworker who just moved to town and doesn't know anyone.

The quiet classmate in your math class.

The neighbor you pass on your way to work every day but never stop and talk to.

Love them! Stop overlooking people. Even for just five minutes. Love them extravagantly. Surprise yourself with how much you can make them feel like the cherished people they already are in Jesus's eyes— uniquely made with a purpose from God!

Struggling to find the treasure that God has buried inside of others? Dig deep. Look for the aspects of God in those people. Ask questions. Have them share their stories with you. Keep digging until you find the unique gifts God has given them. They're in there somewhere!

Want to love someone extravagantly? Ask yourself one simple question: What can I do to make this person feel special? And then go do it! It doesn't always need to be something fancy or shiny; you don't need to go out and give away new cars like Oprah or buy them Starbucks for life (even though that would be awesome!). Simply love the unseen people in your life with what you already have, just as Antonio loves me—extravagant in his own way.

5

Tyler and Travis

Love stays when everyone else leaves.

My two closest friends are two guys named Tyler and Travis. One is a realtor, and the other is a pastor I work with. Tyler and Travis don't really run in the same circles, but I've known them both for years, and they've shown me what love looks like in more ways than I can count.

I first met Tyler while we were in college. We'd see each other here and there but never got to know each other very well. A few years later, when the idea of starting a church first came about, I was living in Kentucky, more than a thousand miles away. One night I randomly reached out to Tyler, who lived in Sioux Falls, to see if he would be interested in attending a new church in town there. He barely knew who I was, yet he said yes when I invited him to a church that didn't have a name and didn't even exist yet.[1]

A few months passed. I moved back to South Dakota, and we started to flesh out the plans for Embrace. Tyler and I started meeting a couple times each month to encourage and spur each other on. His family was one of the first to call Embrace home. From day one, Tyler and his family jumped in. Faithfully giving. Faithfully serving. And for me personally, faithfully lifting me up.

Almost immediately, Tyler's relationship with Jesus inspired me. Seeing his radical generosity inspired me. Seeing his willingness to help people inspired me. Yes, Tyler's a realtor, and I give him a hard time about the countless billboards around town that have a giant picture of his face on them.[2] But he's become a pastor to so many. People often go to him for advice, a listening ear, and prayer. If a businessperson is struggling with a trial, in his marriage, or in his walk with God, I always tell him to meet with Tyler. I know he will be encouraged.

As a rookie pastor, I was so thankful to have a safe place where I could share the good, the bad, and the otherwise, a place where I could be honest, where I could have someone pray for me.

Beginning with that first season of starting the church, Tyler has shown me that love shows up. Love listens. When a friend can't walk, love carries them. Love stays.

There are certain people in your life whom you feel like you'll never be able to repay for their friendship and encouragement. Tyler is one of those people for me. Travis is another.

When Embrace was a couple of years old, we started growing like crazy. Everything was great! Except *me.* I was exhausted, and even though the church was doing well, I was struggling with depression, anxiety, and being totally overwhelmed.[3] We had a handful of amazing part-time staff, and our volunteers were fantastic, but often I still felt completely alone.

One day I hit the end of what I could do. After being a workaholic for three straight years, I was a disaster! I knew something had to change. I needed help. I desperately needed a lifeline. That's when we hired Travis, the first full-time staff person to come work alongside me.[4] He had started coming to Embrace about three years in, and his first day there was actually the Sunday we started meeting in our own space for the first time—the day we began exploding as a church. He quickly got connected and began serving the church any way he could.

Travis was a godsend. When we hired him, it was clear I was no longer alone. He was *with* me, right there cheering me on. Encouraging me. Fighting for me. Praying for me.

Some days, it felt like he was carrying me when I couldn't walk.

But his love was tough too. He pushed back on me, asking me if this or that was really the right move. He made sure we had thought through all the options. He voiced his opinion, speaking into me. His loyalty wasn't only for my comfort, it was for my good. And for the good of the church.

We were both in the trenches. Looking back, we were able to accomplish so much more together than I ever could have on my own. The church was no longer a burden to me. Instead it was a blessing again, and we began to see God move in ways we had never imagined.

People often tell me about how a message I've shared has impacted their life. In the past six years, there's maybe been only one or two messages that Travis hasn't helped shape in a big way. He knows the Bible better than anyone, but even more so he lives it out. He's the real deal!

Both Travis and Tyler have encouraged me and pushed me closer to Jesus for years. But a few summers ago, I went through one of the hardest seasons of my life, a season when I didn't know who was there for me and who wasn't. I've been through some hard seasons before but nothing like this.

I had to make a difficult decision at the church, and it wasn't a popular one. I took six months trying to figure out if there was any way around it. I knew the decision wouldn't be well received, but I never expected the response to be what it was. It was hard. Brutal, actually. (Have you ever had to make a hard decision that you knew you had to make? Ever been misunderstood? There are few things worse.)[5]

Word spread quickly about the decision, but the worst part were the rumors that spread that just weren't true. A few people came and asked me questions, and even if they ultimately disagreed, most understood. But a lot of people walked away without ever asking any questions. People I had known and loved for a decade walked out—not just out of the church but also out of their friendship with me. Without saying a word. I was devastated!

When so many other people distanced themselves from me—people who had really seen only good in me—Tyler and Travis got closer. Even though they had seen the good, bad, and ugly in me.

Through this season, these two guys carried me, both at different times and in their own individual ways. Daily I wanted to give up. Daily I wanted to quit. Daily I wanted to leave the church. I even considered no longer being a pastor. But they wouldn't let me quit.[6]

When I say they carried me, I mean I was on the phone multiple times a day with at least one of them, asking for prayer. Asking for advice. But more than anything, asking them to help me take another step and put one foot in front of the other. There were days I felt completely paralyzed. I was so tired I couldn't pray. I struggled to feel anything. At times I hurt so much, I couldn't even put into words what I was feeling. I felt feelings of bitterness and betrayal that I never knew existed. I wondered if normal would ever return—if the trial I was walking through, that had lasted for months, would ever come to an end.

Each time I called, they answered.

Each time I needed someone to listen, they listened.

They let me share whatever was inside me and didn't judge me.

They helped me see things from a different perspective, which I couldn't see through my hurt and confusion.

As human beings, regardless of who or where we are, we need others. We need other people around us. Studies have shown that people who have good friendships are happier, have fewer health problems, have drastically lower mental health issues, and live longer than people who don't have a good community around them.[7]

Translation: if you have friends, you don't have to exercise ever again, you can pretty much eat anything you want, and you will live forever! Awesome, right? I wish it worked that way. But particularly in the hard times, in the crap and trials of life, we need other people.

Each day, one day at a time, Tyler and Travis pulled me closer to Jesus, simply by staying close to me.[8] They did all they could and then some, and *they were there.* In a season when I couldn't get myself to Jesus—when I felt I couldn't speak or pray—it was Tyler and Travis who got me to Jesus. And they didn't just bring me to Jesus; in so many ways, these two *were* Jesus to me. Their love stayed, when so many others left.

• • •

One of my favorite stories about Jesus involves five friends.[9] Jesus had been teaching and healing people all over the place, and he's now returning to the city of Capernaum, which was his home base at this point in his life.

Jesus went to a house (some think it's where his friend Peter lived), and the news quickly spread that Jesus was there. Out of nowhere, waves of people started showing up because they wanted to see him and see what the fuss was all about. A huge crowd gathered, including a group of four friends carrying their paralyzed buddy on a mat because he couldn't walk. Listen to what happened next:

> Some men came, bringing to him a paralyzed man, carried by four of them. Since they could not get him to Jesus be-cause of the crowd, they made an opening in the roof above Jesus by digging through it and then lowered the mat the man was lying on. When Jesus saw their faith, he said to the paralyzed man, "Son, your sins are forgiven."

That's a pretty crazy scene, right? Because the four guys couldn't get their friend to Jesus, they decided to cut a hole in the roof of a house and lower their buddy in, just so they could get him near Jesus.[10] Yet, get this—when they do it, Jesus heals him!

Jesus tells him, "Stand up, pick up your mat, and go home!"

Their master plan worked. Their friend was miraculously healed. They got the Friends of the Century award right then, for sure.

Yeah, this story is an insanely awesome example of a miracle Jesus performed, but the story of the man and his friends also tells us something about what love should look like—a love I've seen time and again in my own life, a love Tyler and Travis showed me during the most difficult time of my life: a love that stays.

Don't miss it: there were tons of people at this house where Jesus was, yet only four people helped the man on the mat. Only four people noticed. Only four people cared enough to do something. Only four people stayed.

Have you ever felt this way? Have you ever stood in the crowd of people and felt completely invisible?

I never cease to be amazed by how many Facebook friends we can have, yet many of us don't have one friend we can call when we're struggling. Not one person we can sit with when we're hurting. Not one person to keep us on the right path when we're tempted. Not one person who stays when we make a mistake.

We're so "connected," yet we don't have one other person who will show up when we most need someone to be there. One person to show up when no one else does.

There are few greater blessings in this life than having dear friends. The people who answer the phone and just listen. The people who come over when they say they're coming over. The people who help you out when you need someone. The people who are just *there*. You don't need to impress them. You can just *be* with them.

Do you have anyone in your life like this? People who will show up? Sometimes we don't realize our deep need until we're faced with frustrating circumstances, a huge crowd, an unexpected trial, an extremely hard season. Until we're face to face with the unimaginable.

We all need people like this, but we also need to *be* people like this. People who will do what the four men did for their friend on the mat, doing absolutely anything necessary to get their friend to Jesus.

Do you have people like that?[11] Are you that person to others?

If you don't have people like this right now, don't get discouraged or think this chapter doesn't apply to you. Be the kind of person who has a love that stays despite the circumstances. Ever heard the phrase "you have to be a friend to have a friend"? It might sound cheesy, but it's so true. Even if you don't have friends like this in your life yet, you can still be that friend in someone else's life. Taking the initiative to stay instead of leaving is a sure way to build that kind of community around you.[12]

When others leave, love stays.

It stays with people when it's uncomfortable.

It's easy to love others when life is easy. But it's much more difficult when you don't know what to say or how to help others through their situations. Staying can look different in each relationship, but I've found that a love that stays requires a few things.

Have the hard conversations. We typically run from anything that's difficult. But staying with someone and loving her in a difficult season will require a lot of difficult conversations. Ask the hard questions. Have the awkward conversations. And don't leave!

Pray. Sometimes there isn't anything you can do for someone, particularly in a hard season. All you can do is pray. Pray for him regularly. Pray *in person.* Pray whenever he comes to mind. Pray, pray, and pray some more.

Stand with that person. Privately and publicly. Stick your neck out for her.

Encourage. One of the greatest gifts we can offer another person is encouragement. Help him see beyond today. Today might suck, but it will get better. When he has no hope, give him hope. With Jesus, we always have hope! So, look to Jesus. Point others to him. Tomorrow, the sun will come up!

Finally, if at all possible, help that person take the next step. We might not be able to solve everything, but we can help someone move forward. Show up and help her through that difficult season, help her see what the next step is, and help her take it!

These aren't easy things to do (far from it!), but each is a key ingredient to practicing a love that stays with people no matter what they're going through. Love is quick to trust what it knows to be true about a person rather than listening to what others are saying about that person. Staying is hard. Leaving is way easier, and we all know it. But speaking from experience, there's nothing like having people in your life who stay, who love with that kind of love. And really, there's nothing like loving other people like that too.

. . .

I learned a lot of things through that tough season a few summers ago. It was a time of pruning, and honestly, it was really painful.[13] But one of the biggest things I learned was that you can make it through anything if you have a few good friends around you. When you're hurting, when you're scared, when you can't make it to Jesus, you need people who will pick you up and get you to him—right where you needed to be all along.

Tyler and Travis carried my mat during that season and, really, many seasons before and since. Through it all, they've taught me what the story of the paralyzed man and his four friends has taught so many of us: love stays when everyone else leaves. Real love is present. It doesn't back away when things get hard. In fact, it works *harder*, doing whatever it takes, dragging us no matter how thick the crowd, no matter how hard the decision.

Even if a roof gets in our way.

6

Laurent

Love doesn't generalize.

My wife, Bec, and I live in the heart of Sioux Falls—the Cathedral District. If you ever fly into town, you'll see a big old Catholic church on the hill. We're just a few blocks away. At one point, this neighborhood was the center of town. Businesspeople, politicians, and doctors all lived there. But as the town grew, people moved on to newer areas. The Cathedral District was left behind.

Today, families are starting to move back into the neighborhood.[1] Homes are being restored. Something I hope never changes, though, is the diversity of the neighborhood. If you walk the streets, you'll see remarkable things. A banker might live next to a rental that's falling apart. A doctor might be talking over the fence to a single mom who may not have made it through high school. Our neighborhood has the full range of races, languages, and backgrounds. It's unique. It's beautiful. I can't imagine living anywhere else.

The other day, I saw a lady walking through the neighborhood. As I watched from inside my house, I quickly noticed she was so drunk that she could barely stand. I could see her staggering down the sidewalk as she got closer. Sadly, this is a fairly normal occurrence. At least a couple of times each week, people stumble through on the sidewalks.

Despite being completely intoxicated, she was still somehow able to get over to one of the young trees in my front yard. I planted the maple tree and a couple of others a few summers back.[2] She grabbed it to keep herself from falling, the tree bending until she was able to regain her balance. Once she was steadier on her feet, she apparently decided to break the tree off—or at least try her best. She pulled on the skinny trunk of the tree with all her might, using her entire body weight, swaying back and forth with the tree as hard as she could.

Now I'm not sure exactly when it happened, but at some point I became a tree hugger. Maybe it was the three years I spent living in Kentucky surrounded by beautiful, one-hundred-year-old trees, or maybe it was something else entirely. Either way, I'm now one of *those* people. I love plants, flowers—all of it, including trees.

Especially trees.

Back to the lady. She bobbed and weaved like some kind of MMA fighter, twisting and pulling that little tree, trying to break it and beat it up. She was going full "George Washington" on it, trying to chop down my cherry tree. And me? I was mad!

Typically, my heart hurts for the people who frequently stumble down our neighborhood sidewalks during the middle of the day. I'm usually quick to say hello and show kindness, but not this time. As I watched her yank and swing on my tree, my blood boiled. *Why is this drunk lady trying to kill my tree?!*

I ran outside. There was a part of me that wanted to yell, even to throw something at her, to get her to quit vandalizing my property. But before I could do so, she started stumbling away. I still didn't feel sorry for her. At all. The only thing I felt was anger. *Get away from my tree, drunk lady! And don't come back!*

An hour passed after the attempted tree mauling. I had just started to cool down a bit when my eight-year-old daughter, Grayson, came up to me.

"Hey, Dad. Wanna go around the block and pick up trash for fun?" (Yes, we have some strange hobbies in the Weber family.)[3] I said yes—even though I secretly didn't want to.

We got our garbage bags, found the wagon, and started to walk the block. We filled up bags and bags of trash: small, empty vodka bottles; used needles; condoms; half-smoked cigarettes. Just about everything you can imagine, we picked up.

I mumbled as we went. I wasn't just upset with the lady who shook my tree; in this moment I was angry at *all* our neighbors who apparently felt the need to leave our block worse than they found it. I was tired. It seemed like I constantly had to pick up the trash of the people passing by. Didn't they know better? What would they think if I walked by their houses and dropped my trash on *their* front lawns? Did *they* have small trees I could randomly attack?

What was happening in my heart? The actions of one neighbor in a moment of weakness made me doubt the character of all of my neighbors. One negative action changed my opinion of the whole neighborhood. This is generalization at its worst. I stereotyped the entire neighborhood based off of one person.

We went on, past houses and front lawns that reflected the diversity of my neighborhood. Near the end of our walk—only a few houses from home—an elderly African man slowly approached me and Grayson. At first, he spoke to me in French. Not sure how to reply, I quickly said, "We're kinda crazy, just out picking up trash for fun!"

He switched to broken English. "This is not crazy," he said, looking at our trash bags. "This is *love*. It's beautiful!"

He introduced himself as Laurent. He was a neighbor I didn't know we had, even though his house was only three down from ours. After we shook hands, he smiled and walked off.

"This is love. This is love. Beautiful, this is love. Love!" he repeated quietly to himself.

What a humbling moment. Laurent didn't know about the woman who had tried to break off my tree, but he spoke words my soul needed to hear. Laurent showed me that love doesn't generalize. Love doesn't let the actions of one person define your view of others. Love doesn't condemn because of one incident. Love isn't always warm fuzzies and happy feelings. At times, love looks more like picking up the trash of people who seem unworthy of that act of service.

Laurent's unexpected kind words took away my sharp feelings of anger, replacing them with a new idea of love and a refreshed view of how to love the people around me.

. . .

Although Jesus never had someone try to assault his favorite tree (or maybe someone did and we just don't know about it), he does know a thing or two about a love that doesn't generalize.

One of the most well-known stories of all time is about a woman caught in adultery.[4] At this specific time, cheating on your husband was an offense punishable by death. I think most would agree that cheating isn't a good thing to do—but punishing it with death? That's a little harsh! A group of people had caught the woman and brought her to Jesus, reminding him that the Jewish law at the time said she deserved death and must be stoned for this crime.

Trying to corner Jesus, the people asked, "What do you think should happen to her?" They hoped Jesus would say something contrary to the law. But instead of answering them, Jesus stooped down and wrote something in the sand with his finger.[5]

The group of guys continued to want an answer, so finally Jesus stood up and told them, "All right, but let the one who has never sinned throw the first stone!"

Nobody moved. Nobody threw a rock. Instead, one by one, the people heard his words and began to walk away, leaving Jesus standing alone with the woman. Each of them knew they had screwed up at one point or another, and Jesus had called them out on it. As my kids would say, "Boom, roasted!"

After they all had left, Jesus turned to the woman and said, "Where are your accusers? Didn't even one of them condemn you?"

"No, Lord."

"Neither do I. Go and sin no more."

Jesus didn't assume or generalize. He didn't have to. He saw the best in this woman even when the crowd saw only the worst. Instead of seeing her as a person, the people accusing her based all of their thoughts on one embarrassing decision she had made—just like I had summed up all of a woman's life by one action and not just her life but the lives of all of my neighbors as well. Jesus's love, on the flip side, has no conditions. It doesn't generalize based on the worst version of a person or on the most shameful thing she's done. Instead, love looks for the best, seeing the good within. Jesus looked at the woman as a child of God. She had made a mistake, but she wasn't defined by it.

It's possible that the woman left Jesus that day only to go out and cheat on her husband again. People will let you down. But that possibility didn't change how Jesus saw her and treated her when he spoke with her. Most likely, though, the woman didn't go back to cheating on her husband; my guess is that she was changed. Jesus loved her so well. So unexpectedly. I'd like to think that Jesus seeing the best in her made her want to become the woman Jesus knew she could be. Jesus saw the best version of her. He chose to base his love off that best, not off her worst.

Jesus didn't generalize.

• • •

It's easy to get upset and judge a person based on that one thing that hurt you. The one time you crossed paths and it wasn't pretty. The one action that made you mad. That's what I did that day with the lady who tried to body-slam the tree in my front yard. That's what the crowd of people did with the cheating woman. I let the tree lady's one action impact the way I saw her, and for a few hours I let it impact the way I saw a whole group of people. Have you ever done that? Have you ever based your thoughts about a group of people off the actions of one? Ever generalized? I was angry at all my neighbors, who—in my irrational view—were messing up the neighborhood, not just the one lady.

But just because the lady attacked my tree, it doesn't mean all my neighbors go around MMA fighting other people's trees. Instead, the majority are like Laurent, the man who appreciated the beauty of picking up some trash. They remind me what wonderful people my neighbors really are.

When we practice a love that doesn't generalize, we end up seeing people for who they truly are, not who we've assumed they are. Life is so much more interesting this way, when we don't paint people with that broad brush of generalization. Generalization slowly makes us blind to people and all the unique and awesome things about them.

In a time when so much of our culture is full of black-and-white over-generalized thinking, this kind of love is radical. It sets us apart from the talking heads we see on TV and listen to online. It refuses to take the easy way out and truly sees others, just as Jesus did that day when he wrote in the sand, refusing to see the woman as just another sinner and instead seeing her as the person she really was. Yeah, she screwed up, but her story wasn't done yet!

Sometimes practicing a love that doesn't generalize starts with our actions, knowing that our hearts will follow. I started picking up trash with my daughter, and my heart followed. My heart changed with a little—okay, a lot—of help from Laurent and my then-eight-year-old daughter.

Jesus didn't need to physically do something to feel love for the woman caught in adultery. His love is perfect, after all. But he did model that action-to-heart practice of loving the best version of someone, not the worst, for us. Even if we're not "feeling it," when we begin doing something for another person, our hearts often will get to a place where we genuinely love people for the best they have to offer, not settling for the generalization we have in our heads.

Are you struggling to focus on the best version of people, not the worst? Struggling to really see people? Remember all the times you've screwed up. I can look back on any given week and see all the times I've messed things up. I would only hope that people wouldn't sum up who I am and generalize other people like me (men, pastors, dads) based on the worst version of myself.

In the Bible, fellow Christians are called "brothers and sisters"—so treat people like brothers and sisters.[6] You don't believe the worst about your brother or sister. At least you shouldn't. Rather than believing the worst about someone, look past the surface and see if there's something deeper going on. Ask questions. Try and find out more about a person's story.

Refrain from generalizations and black-and-white thinking in general. Nobody (and no group of people) is all good or all bad. They're almost always somewhere in between. We like to generalize and label things. We like to put people in small boxes, but we can't, and we shouldn't.

Laurent's gentle words "this is love" showed me that God can use me to love others well in any circumstance, even when I'm doing so begrudgingly, as I was with the neighborhood cleanup. You may not see it or even really notice, but God is using you right now to love other people.

The more we love others, the more God will shape our hearts to look like his, to look for the things in others that he looks for. Love doesn't look for a person's screwups. Instead, like Jesus, it notices and celebrates the very best that is inside of that person.

Love doesn't generalize. It really *sees*.

So should we.

7

Brett

Love heals through unlikely people.

Brett and I have known each other for years, but truthfully, it seems like Brett has known just about everyone for years.[1] No matter the setting he's in, people are drawn to him.

Brett is a guy who's willing to try anything and everything—skiing, lacrosse, horseback riding, water tubing, hockey, you name it. Other than horseback riding, I've never done any of those things myself.[2]

But more than anything, Brett is someone I look up to, respect, and appreciate so much.

Something else to know about Brett? It's almost a side note to me: he has been in a wheelchair his entire life.

Born with cerebral palsy, he has limited use of his arms and hands. He has some strength but no balance. His speech is slurred. Even after years of knowing Brett, I often have to ask him to repeat sentences so I can understand him. Sometimes he has to repeat a sentence a few times. Physically, Brett's body is broken. Things don't work as they should.

Another part of Brett's story? His birth mother, due to being young and not in a situation to provide for a child, gave him up for adoption.[3] He was adopted by an amazing set of parents who didn't know he had cerebral palsy until Brett was a few months old. They began to realize he wasn't able to do things other babies could, but it didn't change anything for them—they continued to love him. To this day, Brett's parents are an active part of Brett's daily life and schedule even though he is now thirty-eight years old.

If there was ever a person with an excuse to call it quits, be angry at God, or, at the very least, coast through life, it would be Brett. But then Brett wouldn't be *Brett*. Instead, Brett lives each day to the fullest. Where others would see obstacles, he sees opportunities.

He's a spokesperson who travels throughout the state, speaking up for others with disabilities.

He's started a business.

He graduated from a university with honors.

He serves on boards.

He plays on sports teams.[4]

But more than anything, he *loves* people and his joy is impossible to miss.

Over the years, Brett has challenged me to not play life safe. To take risks. To step out. To see opportunities and ignore limitations. To be used by God.

Recently, we met at Josiah's, one of my favorite lunch spots downtown.[5] I helped Brett use ramps to enter the building. I placed his order, knowing the person behind the counter would struggle to understand his words. And when we got to our table, I cut up his food and put a straw in his drink.

To anyone watching, Brett appeared to be the broken person who needed help. But little did they know, I was the broken person—the one who needed help, the one who needed to be made whole.

Brett asked how I was doing that day, and I shared that I was going through a hard time, a season of uncertainty and pain as I walked through a series of health scares with my parents on top of a really busy time at work. I felt really broken. He listened and listened and *listened.* After not saying anything for a while, Brett spoke words of truth into my life that I'll never forget:

"Adam, you're so loved."

"Adam, God is using you."

"Adam, God can be trusted."

At the very end, Brett said, "When we do things our way, they never work out. But when we do things God's way, they go so much better." So true!

I didn't need to hear a grand speech. Just a few simple words. Words I so badly needed to hear that day, and, really, every day since. Brett's words started a shift that began to change my outlook. Slowly, very slowly, I went from being angry at God—questioning him and his plan, asking, *Why would you let this happen?*—to realizing that I had been trying to do things my way, paddling against the current, and it wasn't working out.

Brett is limited and I'm the healthy one. Or at least that's what it looked like on the outside that day. But on the inside, Brett was the strong one and I was the one needing help. Sure, I helped Brett through the door of the restaurant, but in reality Brett opened the door for me—a door to a new way of seeing God's hand in my circumstances. I helped Brett order his meal and eat his lunch, but he helped me find God in my broken mess. I'll never be able to repay him for that. Through all of his disabilities, Brett loved me by revealing my own brokenness and then helping me start the process of healing.

• • •

There's one person Jesus encountered who's different from all the rest. Many approached Jesus for healing, to hear his teachings, or to be near him, but only one person came to Jesus after he was cruci-fied—a man named Joseph from a town called Arimathea.

Now, before we move on, we need to remember that while Jesus was human and he walked on earth, he was also fully God. Let me say that again: Jesus is God! Holy. Set apart. Unlike *anyone* else.

Jesus is the Creator. He has no beginning or end. Not just a king but the King of kings. Not just a lord but the Lord of lords. He walked on water, healed people, calmed storms, brought the dead back to life.

Joseph was a man. Jesus is God, the Son of man.

Joseph had a powerful position. Jesus is all-powerful (and all-knowing and all-present).

Joseph knew about truth. Jesus *is* the Truth.

But Jesus died. His lifeless body was hanging on the cross, and his body had to get to the tomb. Surely the King of kings and the Lord of lords would have a legion of angels that would supernaturally carry his body to the tomb, right? Wouldn't a royal parade take him there? Nope. No angels, no parade, just one person. One man who was also part of the same crowd that led to Jesus being killed in the first place.

This man named Joseph was the one who took Jesus's body to its "final" resting place. Yet the unlikelihood of the situation (a simple man caring for an all-powerful God) doesn't stop Joseph from com-ing and ministering to Jesus. Jesus had just died a horrible death, and Joseph wanted to make sure that Jesus's body would be taken care of with dignity. Joseph saw Jesus's broken body and wanted to help.

When you begin to fully understand the power that Jesus possessed by being God, you realize that Joseph was an unlikely person to bury Jesus's body. When Jesus had been abandoned by all, when he was fully broken and dead, angels didn't show up. Joseph did. That's unexpected.

Joseph, this unlikely man, stepped in. He played a part in God's bigger plan for Jesus's resurrection. Joseph boldly approached Pilate, the Roman ruler, and asked for Jesus's body, and Pilate allowed him to take it to be buried.

Now, listen to what Joseph did next: "Then he took it down, wrapped it in linen cloth and placed it in a tomb cut in the rock, one in which no one had yet been laid."[6]

Maybe you should read that verse one more time.

Joseph, who was just a willing person, maybe not even one of Jesus's followers at the time of Jesus's death, went up to the cross, took down the body of God from where he was hanging, wrapped him in a clean cloth, and buried him in a brand-new tomb. Some accounts even suggest that this was Joseph's own tomb, set aside for his burial.

Joseph, a very unlikely person, ministered to God himself.

. . .

No matter who you are, at some point you'll be broken. Even the Son of God was broken. Even the Son of God died. You'll also feel your humanity. You'll feel like you're the most unlikely person to ever be used by God. Maybe you'll be broken in small ways here and there or be broken in big ways. Ways that you're sure you'll never fully recover from. Even Jesus needed someone to care for him when he was broken. You need someone to care for you, too, no matter what kind of brokenness you're walking through.

Whether you're a pastor, teacher, counselor, parent, leader, whatever, you're a human being with a soul. Recently I grabbed coffee with an important city leader. After some small talk, he said, "Everyone expects me to be perfect all the time, and I'm anything but. For months, I've been struggling with depression, and it's embarrassing! Adam, that's why I'm reaching out to you." At some point, we all need others to care for us. And when you need care, just as Jesus did, God will often use unlikely people to serve you in your time of need.

The person who may appear unlikely and broken—like my friend Brett—may actually be the one who can help, while the person who appears whole and "qualified" may actually be the one who *needs* help.

Brett was in a wheelchair and needed help to eat his lunch. Some would say he's the very definition of broken, yet he ministered to me. Brett healed *my* hurt and *my* jaded heart during that hour-long lunch. He healed, not despite his brokenness, but because of it.

Love heals through the most unlikely of people.

No one is more qualified to love than the unlikely person. In fact, our past or present "disqualifications" actually put us in a more likely position to be relatable to others. We are better at recognizing the pain in their eyes. When a person realizes we're not perfect—and far from it—he's much more willing to confide in us and trust us. Take a lesson from my friend Brett: life is too short to play it safe. Even if you feel unlikely, step out. Take risks. Practice a love that heals in the most unlikely of ways. Nine times out of ten, those limitations make you more qualified to love, not less.

But how do we love when we feel so unlikely to be used? Begin to realize that God doesn't create accidents. Whatever happened to you, whatever your story is, God wants to use it! Whether God caused something or simply allowed it to take place, he knew about it long before you did. He not only can use it but wants to use it for your good and the good of others.

Often for God to use our unlikeliness, we need to start by stopping. Stop blaming others for where you are. Stop feeling sorry for yourself and start stepping out. Blaming others and feeling sorry for yourself will kill all the ways God wants to use you. Instead of being used by God, you'll simply remain angry at him, unable to see the good that could come from your story.

When you start stepping out, you'll begin looking for ways to match your deepest area of unlikeliness to a ministry or group of people who need to hear from you. You'll tell them how you stopped—

stopped complaining, stopped feeling sorry for yourself, stopped blaming God—so that you could start living again.

So, as you think of your unlikeliness, your brokenness, your wounds, your pain, your failures, ask yourself, *How can I use what looks like weakness, woundedness, or even unlikeliness to heal others as Jesus would?* When you answer that, you'll be living like Brett and Joseph.

Because love heals through the most unlikely of people. And it always has.

8

Rick and Val

Love comforts through the worst.

When I was a sophomore in high school, my family switched churches and Tara was one of the first people I met at our new church. Back then I didn't want anything to do with God, and I was counting down the Sundays until I started college and wouldn't have to go to church anymore. But Tara was fun and cool. She and the friends she hung out with were so different from anyone else I knew, and I wanted to find out more.[1]

Soon Tara began inviting me to hang out with a group of friends who typically met at her family's house. Each time, I was thrilled to be included. Part of me still felt like that unpopular kid from elementary school, so every time I was invited somewhere, I said yes!

Whenever I went to Tara's, I would start the night by hanging out in the basement with all the other high school kids my age; then, at some point, I'd wander upstairs to talk with Tara's parents, Rick and Val. I'm not really sure why, but there was just something about them that I was drawn to.

Rick was a well-respected superintendent at the local school. My mom was an associate principal in the same district and practically worshipped the ground Rick walked on. She loved working for such an honest, encouraging person. I would often see Rick on his morning run around town, running what looked like a marathon before most people were even out of bed! I only hoped to someday be as sharp looking and respected as he was. (Maybe in heaven, when I get a new heavenly body, I will be a runner?[2])

Val was fun and over the top. She didn't care who you were or where you were from; she loved everyone. Her personality was contagious. She talked about Jesus like he was physically in the room—something I had never experienced before.

Rick and Val were life-givers. They showed me that a person could love Jesus and have a blast doing so. At first glance, I assumed their lives were perfect.

But after getting to know Tara more, I soon discovered that the image I had of them wasn't the whole story. While Val was still in college, she had become pregnant with Tara. Val's dad, Gordie, was the head basketball coach at that same college—a Christian college.[3] Gordie was also the guy who helped bring the Fellowship of Christian Athletes to the state of South Dakota. In local terms, he was a pretty big deal in the Christian world.

Getting pregnant in college, particularly at that time, was frowned on for anyone's daughter, let alone the daughter of a well-known Christian coach and leader. Val didn't expect the pregnancy, and she wasn't prepared. She was embarrassed about getting pregnant and wasn't ready to be a mom. She secretly hoped she wouldn't carry the baby to term. But she did, and for that I'm so thankful. If it hadn't been for Tara, I wouldn't have met Rick and Val—and honestly, my life would look so different than it does today.

Val was a young, twenty-year-old single mom when she ran into Rick. Without hesitation, Rick stepped into the picture, married Val, and became Tara's father. To this day, their family story is still one of my favorites. An unplanned pregnancy and Tara's adoption weren't the only bumps Rick and Val would encounter together.

• • •

High school passed for me, then college. I met and married my wife, Bec, and for some reason I decided I wanted to become a pastor. (I'm still a little stunned this is what I do for a job, just being honest.) I decided to go to seminary in Kentucky. Bec and I had no idea how we were going to make ends meet. We were *barely* covering the basics of school, gas, and food, and we had very little extra, almost nothing. Newly married, I was a full-time student while Bec was working part-time making minimum wage.[4] It was a wonderful season of life, but the constant financial stress was a cloud that never seemed to go away.

Early on in our time in Kentucky, my car needed its brakes repaired. I tried to get by without fixing them, but there's only so far one can make it with bad brakes on winding Kentucky back roads. We had to cut our spending back even further. But one day, out of nowhere, we got a letter in the mail from Rick and Val. Inside was a check for one hundred dollars. Bec and I thanked God—then we practically ran to the grocery store.[5] What an unexpected blessing! We couldn't believe it!

But it wasn't over. Next month came. We got another unexpected letter in the mail from Rick and Val with another hundred dollars. Next month too—and the one after that. And so on.

Every month for three years.

During that same time, Rick and Val were rocked by tragedy. Their son, who was then a freshman in high school, was out driving with a friend one day. Their son stopped at a stop sign, looked both ways, and pulled out onto the highway, not seeing a motorcycle carrying a man and woman. The motorcycle struck Rick and Val's son's car, and the man was killed. A tragedy like that takes a toll on every single life involved, no matter who or where they were at the time.

Years passed, and Bec and I ended up in Sioux Falls to start Embrace. A little while later, Rick and Val moved to Sioux Falls, too, and were looking for a church. Embrace really didn't have anyone their age. Our "old people" were in their forties, while Rick and Val were in their fifties. Ancient, right? I kid. I couldn't meet with them fast enough.

"Don't feel any pressure to attend," I said, "but we'd love to have you. You don't have to do anything. On Sundays just come and stand in our entryway so other 'older' people can feel like they belong here. You'll be like missionaries to people around your age!"

Rick and Val started coming—and immediately they brought their friends! Others in their fifties and up could relate to them. Turns out they were missionaries, not just to people of their own age but to all ages. Their openness and wisdom made them the kind of people others wanted to be around. Over the years, Rick and Val have met with single moms, young couples struggling with marriage, parents, and everyone else. I tell pretty much anyone who will listen, particularly those walking through a difficult time in life, "You need to meet with these people. Do anything you can to meet up. Pay for their coffee, their meal. You'll be better for meeting with Rick and Val!"

A few years passed. Another trial came ripping through their lives. Rick had continued to climb every career ladder imaginable in education, going from superintendent of a large school to secretary of education for the state of South Dakota, to dean of education for the University of South Dakota. He became a consultant, desiring to help and share his expertise with others.

Everything was going well. Until it wasn't. Rick didn't do anything wrong, but one of his clients had been embezzling money. That man ended up taking his own life—along with the lives of his entire family. It was shocking. Horrible. Heartbreaking.

Of course, it made the news. The story was everywhere. One of the bigger news outlets brought Rick's name into the story. In a matter of hours, Rick was now tied to this horrible event. His name was brought up daily. Weeks turned into months and months turned into years, but the story didn't go away, and Rick went from being one of the most respected people in the state to one surrounded by controversy. Longtime friends and connections walked away. Opportunities disappeared. His reputation and his family's were now up in the air.

Little did I know, a trial was about to come my own way.

Although it was nothing compared to what Rick went through, I also walked through a season when my character and reputation were called into question: the summer when Tyler and Travis showed me how love stays. Like I said before, many of the things that were shared about me just weren't true. Being in a place of leadership, I couldn't really say anything, and trying to defend myself would have only made things worse.[6] People I had known, served, and loved for ten-plus years walked out of my life without asking a single question or wanting to know if there was more to the story. I was devastated. As someone who only wants to do good and help people, I was at a loss for words when others questioned what felt like the very basics about me.

Through it all, Rick and Val were with me. Time and time again, on Sundays and throughout the week, we'd cross paths and they would encourage me.

"Adam, keep your head up!"

"You're on the right path."

"Anyone in a leadership position has or will walk through something like this."

"Don't let bitterness overtake you."

"We're in your corner!"

One specific morning, Rick shared this with me: "Though you can't control your reputation, you can control your character! Focus on that."

Rick and Val showed me what love looks like in the midst of the worst that life can bring. Instead of running away to take cover, love moves into the open and comforts when we're in the middle of it all. That's what Rick and Val did for me, and that's how they've lived their lives—not despite the worst but *because* of the worst that has come their way.

• • •

One person who wrote a large part of the Bible was a guy named Paul. He built tents for a living.[7] Besides writing a portion of the Bible (no big deal), Paul was used powerfully by God to spread the news about Jesus to anyone who would listen.

Paul was walking on a road to a place called Damascus, when out of nowhere he was blinded by a light, like a deer in the headlights. The light wasn't oncoming traffic, though; it was Jesus. Up until this point, Paul wasn't just not a Christian; he was actively killing Christians.

Paul went from killing Christians to signing people up to *become* Christians. All because of a meetup with the risen Jesus. Paul would go on to write letters to different churches. Near the beginning of his letter to the church in the city of Corinth, Paul wrote this about Jesus: "He comforts us in all our troubles so that we can comfort others."[8]

The word *troubles* here can also translate to mean "trials." When Paul speaks these words, he's not just talking about having a bad day or dealing with traffic on the way to work. He's talking about the trials he faced that almost ended in death—being shipwrecked, beaten, and thrown into a Roman prison, just to name a few.

Most of us have had our own metaphorical shipwreck.

Maybe you've battled cancer.

Maybe you were in a car accident that nearly took your life.

Maybe you lost a parent or close friend.

Maybe you've had rumors spread about you that weren't true.

Maybe you've experienced the worst of life firsthand.

But big or small, we're often tempted to diminish the pain. We think, *I shouldn't complain about my husband's affair while other people are dying. I shouldn't talk about losing my job when I have perfect health and there are others who don't. I shouldn't be upset about someone hurting me when a guy like Paul was physically beaten for his faith.*

Thankfully, though, Paul doesn't give any qualifiers about God comforting us. Our trials don't need to be a "ten" for God to offer his comfort to us. Instead, in all of our troubles and trials, in all of our pain and hurt, God comforts us.

God doesn't diminish our pain. He meets us in it.

Paul goes on to tell us more. Not only does God comfort us in our trials, but those trials also have a purpose: "He comforts us in all our troubles *so that* we can comfort others. When they are troubled, we will be able to give them the same comfort God has given us."[9]

God didn't cause our trials, but he can use them. God can use the crap we've experienced to help others walking through the same crap. Our place of pain can become our place of passion. God can use our hurt to help heal others.

How do we use our hurt to help others heal? Be honest about it. Sadly, the norm in church is to bury our hurt and move forward— forgive and don't process. "If you trusted God, you wouldn't let this hurt bother you." If you survive a storm, you're expected to quickly gather yourself and act like it didn't happen.[10]

Ironically, this approach is the complete opposite of what we find throughout the Bible. Scripture is full of people grieving and lamenting, of processing pain and hurt with God and themselves. Most of us, including myself, could take some notes from this. Yes, we need to forgive. Yes, we need to trust God. But we also need to care for our wounds and make sure they properly heal; otherwise, we'll only keep hurting people and not be able to bring healing to anyone. Caring for our own hurts and wounds is one of the most loving things we can do for the people around us.[11]

In order to help others heal, we need to also be vulnerable.[12] One of the very first things we put on each morning is a mask. A mask to hide any hurt, along with the not-so-pretty parts of our story. A mask to hide the storms we've weathered or are walking through. Being vulnerable takes courage. Speaking from the heart is scary. Letting our guard down and being genuine is hard. It's risky as well! But being vulnerable with others not only brings them healing—by inviting them to be vulnerable too—it also helps bring healing to ourselves.

So, share your story. Throughout this book, we've been talking about people's stories, and the most powerful story we can share (besides Jesus's story) is our own. Everyone has walked through tough times. When we begin to share our honest and unedited stories, it connects us with others. People rarely grow and heal by hearing about our successes and the blue-sky days we've had throughout life. But sharing about the dark skies, the thunder, the sleet, and the fog? That opens the door for others to begin being honest about their own pain and vulnerable about their own hardships. Maybe then they'll start to share their stories and trials with others, bringing healing to those people as well.

God can use our hurt to help heal others. That's what Rick and Val did. It's what they did for Bec and me at so many different points in our lives, and it's what they've done for so many others. They've comforted out of the comfort they've received from God himself. They took their trials and their battle scars and used them for good.

Something Val once said has always stuck with me: "I hate the pain this person is walking through, but God will no doubt use it."

Just to say it again, God doesn't cause our pain, but he does have a divine purpose for it. I've seen this lived out in the lives of Rick and Val, maybe more so than I have in anyone else. The legendary priest Henri Nouwen called this the way of the "wounded healer"—where we become people who teach and heal out of the very places where we've been wounded the most.[13]

Our pain qualifies us to enter into the pain of others. Our trials qualify us to be wounded healers.

When someone is walking through a divorce, the loss of a child, or hurtful gossip, our own pain qualifies us to speak the words "I've been there."

"I know what you're going through."

"It sucks. I know. I'm so sorry."

"I've walked through that too. You're going to make it through."

"You will make it out on the other side."

"The sun will come up tomorrow. I promise."

"God will use even this."

How do I know this is true? Because it's been true in my life.

Are you going through a rough time right now? A season of pain? God has a plan for even this. In our darkest moments, we'll discover the most about Jesus and who he is. Those places are where I've not only discovered his peace that surpasses all understanding but also discovered his love—a love that has no end.

As anyone who's crossed paths with Rick and Val knows, *love* is a word that sums them up so well. Better yet, *Jesus* does.

9

Hudson, Wilson, Grayson, and Anderson

Love doesn't always need words.

When I think of love, some of the first people who come to mind are Hudson, Wilson, Grayson, and Anderson Weber.[1] My kids. And four kids is a lot these days. We're one human away from being able to have our own basketball team![2]

I'm going to be brutally honest, hoping it will encourage someone: until a couple of years ago, being a dad felt more like a job than a blessing. I had to intentionally put my dad-face on to love my kids. *You can do this,* I'd tell myself. It didn't come naturally, and most days I just wanted them to go to bed. Terrible, right? I still regret it.

I'm not sure what changed, but about two years ago something shifted within me. I'm so glad this change took place when my oldest was still a fifth grader. Life goes by so quickly. That fifth grader is now an eighth grader, and time doesn't seem to be slowing down. Coworkers, clients, and even friends will come and go. But as long as they're alive and so are you, your kids will always be your kids.[3] One day I felt God saying to me, "You might want to start treating the most important people in your life like they're the most important instead of the least."

Now, kids can definitely have their not-so-great moments, but generally speaking, one thing little kids do well is love. Kids love unconditionally—their memories seem to reset once every twenty-four hours (most of the time it's more like every twenty-four minutes). Even after my worst week of being a dad, when I get home, my kids can't wait to say hello, throw their arms around me, and just be near me in general.

They don't hold my crabbiness from the day before against me. They don't remember my epic parenting fails (unless it's something we laugh about together later). They don't care about titles or awards.

They simply love me. Fully. Completely. Unconditionally.

Speaking of epic parenting fail moments, I've had many. Lots! But on one particular day that I try to forget, I took it to another level. It was a really hard day. I got a few not-so-fun emails and received a not-so-fun phone call. The people pleaser in me was trying to make everyone happy, and, well, it wasn't working. I felt like a failure. This particular week I had way overbooked myself. On top of feeling like a failure, I was so busy that it seemed as if I didn't even have time to breathe.

Somehow, I survived the day. But on my drive home, instead of catching a short break, I took yet another phone call, which lasted right until I parked my car in our garage. I was exhausted and was hoping for a quiet moment once I got in the house.

But . . . I'm a father of four kids. Our house isn't quiet (it's mass chaos) until everyone is sleeping near the very end of the day, and that time was hours away. Once home, I planned to go into my house and directly up to our bedroom as quickly as I could, locking the door behind me. For my kids' sake—sparing them from seeing what I was feeling in that moment—and also for my own sanity, I just needed a little alone time.

Unfortunately, my plan was a no go. The moment I stepped out of my garage, I was greeted by all four kids. At once. They were playing in the sprinklers in our backyard and shooting one another with squirt guns, having a blast. They were laughing hysterically. It was the picture of joy, fun, and happiness. Cue the cranky old dad! As soon as I exited the garage, I became their primary target, and they started soaking me with water.

Normally, this wouldn't have been a big deal. I'd join in the fun and grab a squirt gun, even if it wasn't planned. But it had been a rough day—a *really* rough day. I got sprayed. Asking them to stop just brought the water on harder and got them more excited to keep spraying me. I could tell they wanted to help, to break me out of my crabbiness by getting me *more* involved in the water fight, but it didn't work. I got sprayed. Again. And out of nowhere it was like I had turned into a dragon. I snapped. As I write this, I'm honestly embarrassed to share the details of what happened next.

In the midst of being sprayed by the water guns that had appeared out of nowhere, I somehow managed to lose one of my shoes. I quickly spotted it—there it was—in a puddle of water. My shoe was soaked. And me? I was now standing in a puddle of water with a fully submerged sock-covered foot. That was the last straw!

What did I do? I picked up the sopping-wet shoe and started hitting it against the ground as hard as I possibly could. Over and over again. I sprayed water and mud everywhere as the shoe hit the earth, yelling as I did. I wasn't directing my anger toward anyone; I was just screaming to let off steam. But let's just pause here and agree this wasn't my best moment as a dad.

But I still had a little lower left to sink. My arm was quickly starting to get tired as I hit the ground with my shoe (I'm getting old). So, I took the shoe, and what did I do? I chucked it! Hard and far. As far as I could! If there was an Olympic event for shot put with footwear, I would have qualified. The shoe sailed over our garage and ended up hitting the side of our neighbor's house!

Yep, I threw my shoe, and it hit our neighbor's house.[4]

Seeing their dad acting like a madman, my kids went from laughing and dancing in the sprinklers to crying their eyes out. Bawling! "Dad, are you okay?" "Dad, what's *wrong*?" They ran into the house to get away from the craziness.

My wife, Becky, needed no words. Her glance said it all. *Who are you?* She followed the kids into the house.

A few minutes passed. I came to my senses a bit. Dripping and shoeless, I walked inside. Embarrassed? Sure. But more than just embarrassed, in that moment I was struggling to process what I was feeling. I lay down, right in the middle of our living room floor, trying to gather my thoughts. I was hurting and exhausted.

"Kids," I asked gently, "can you come over here to me?" All four did. The only words I could get out were "Dad is hurting, and I'm sorry for acting that way."

Without even asking, all of them gathered around and hugged me. Their love didn't need words. It was so honest, so accepting—even after my moment outside.

Each of them touched me with their love, but I'll never forget how my son Wilson responded. Wilson is our adopted son from Ethiopia, and he rarely offers a hug to anyone. Physical touch isn't his thing. He's pretty guarded in general and doesn't show affection often, even to me and Bec. When it comes to hugs, we typically have to chase him down to get one. Literally. But in that moment, he saw me hurting, and he walked up to me and leaned his body into mine. It was the best hug I've ever received from him.

The kids didn't say a word. They didn't tell me I was crazy (until the next day when we laughed about the whole shoe-throwing thing).[5] They didn't hide from me or make me feel like I was insane.

They just loved me.

• • •

At several different points in the Bible, Jesus interacted with kids. His message to anyone listening is the same each time: "Become like them!" On one occasion, parents brought their kids to Jesus in hopes that he would pray for them and bless them.[6] We're not given any names of the parents or their kids, but we are told that those closest to Jesus—his crew, his twelve disciples—began to scold the parents, telling them to stay away, because they didn't want these kids to bother Jesus.

Jesus responded a little differently than the disciples: "Don't stop them! Become like them! Heaven belongs to those who are like these children."

The disciples must have been shocked. These loud, grubby little kids were trying to climb all over Jesus! Jesus had so much on his mind, so much to do. Why would Jesus even want them near him, much less let them touch him? *He has more important people to talk with and more important things to do than deal with a pack of kids, doesn't he?*

Jesus viewed kids much differently, though. He knew that children are naturals at things most adults forget as they get older. Kids are able to love in a pure, unjaded way. Kids forgive instead of hold grudges. Kids trust. They offer second chances.

Once again, kids are far from perfect. But they love without needing words.

As these kids were sitting around Jesus, he told the crowd (along with all of us) that the kingdom of God belongs to these kids—the ones who came to him, sat with him, and believed in him without an agenda, without having to ask for proof.

The kingdom of God belongs to people who have hearts like children and are able to love like little kids. So what does that mean for us shoe throwers? Maybe for us, the first step to remembering how to really love is to allow ourselves to drip on the living room floor while we get hugged. It's about receiving love before we can give it.

• • •

Supposedly the older we get, the wiser we become. But when it comes to love, the opposite appears to be true. Often the older we get, the worse we become at loving people. You don't meet too many judgmental, cynical, defensive, or hurtful little kids. If you do, it's probably because those kids have experienced more of the tough things in life than many adults have.

The kind of love my kids showed to me that summer day when I freaked out and threw the shoe is the same kind of love the kids showed to Jesus. Okay, maybe it was a little easier to love Jesus than it was to love me, but you get the point.

In order to love me the day of the ill-fated water fight, my kids didn't even need to speak. They were just there. Present. When I went inside to lie on the floor and gather my thoughts, my kids didn't rush in and try to tell me what I was feeling or what I should have done differently. Instead they knelt down beside me and sat with me in my hurt. They felt my pain, and I felt their love without them having to say anything at all.

As adults, we need to do this more. So often, we're quick to speak when wanting to show people we love them. We attempt to fix someone or their problems, instead of just being *present.* Sure, at times words are needed, but a lot of times, especially when those we love are hurting, we don't really need to say anything at all.

The unconditional love kids show is constant—present each day, never seeming to waver. Yes, sometimes kids get mad and hold a grudge, but while adult grudges can last years, kids' grudges barely last a few minutes. Their love resets almost as fast as their attention spans, and it's a love that endures over the long haul.

The love that kids have isn't based on what a person does; it's based on who a person is. Kids don't care about titles. My kids could honestly care less if I pastored a church of ten thousand or just our family of six. They don't care how many followers I have on Instagram. They just care that I'm their dad. Kids simply care about the person—not the person's accomplishments, status, or lack thereof.

Hudson, Wilson, Grayson, and Anderson Weber are not perfect examples of love by any means (just come over to our house some night and you'll see), but they have shown me what it means to love like kids do—with a love that's constant, unconditional, and that sees the best in other people. A love that doesn't always need words to show it's there.

. . .

The thing about the day of the shoe throwing that stayed with me the most was actually what happened before I came in the house. After throwing the shoe, my kids all ran into the house, but before I went in, my oldest son, Hudson, came back out into the yard.

"Dad, do you want your shoe?" Before I could stop him, he ran out our backyard gate. "I'll get it, Dad!"

It's something that I'll never forget. In that moment, Hudson was Jesus to me.

In the same way that Hudson went and grabbed my shoe without having to say anything more than "I'll get it, Dad!"—a shoe I should have sheepishly gone after myself—Jesus shows us something very similar through his actions on the cross.

I want to love like a little kid. I want to love like Jesus does, with a love that picks up a shoe, gives a hug, dies on a cross, a love that doesn't always need words to be deeply felt.

10

Becky

Love washes feet.

Bec and I started dating in October of our senior year of college.

Bec was the girl of my dreams.

Kind. Soft spoken. Beautiful.

Thank you, Jesus![1]

We started dating in October and were engaged that December. When you know, you know, right?[2] We were married in North Dakota that next August at the same church where her dad was the pastor.[3] This was also the church where I had first met her while filling in for her dad as an intern pastor the summer before. Friends and family we didn't even know we had showed up to celebrate "the two God had brought together" that day in August 2004. Our wedding day was perfect.

But we quickly found out that married life is anything but perfect. Sometimes the hardest people to love are those closest to you. Siblings so different from you that you can't believe they were created by the same DNA pool that created you. Moms and dads who often behave like children.

Time with family can be wonderful, but it can also be really difficult, filled with hurt, wounds, and history. Family members are people you didn't get to choose; they're just there. Even more than loving the family you didn't get to choose, if there's one place where I've learned about what love is, it's through marriage—the person you *did* choose, which sometimes makes it easier to want to "unchoose" them (along with the in-laws).

Unlike siblings and parents, whom you move away from at some point,[4] your spouse is tied to you financially, emotionally, physically—living under the same roof with you! What starts out as a perfect wedding day quickly becomes two imperfect people attempting to love each other till death do them part. And forever is a long, long time.

The things that initially drew you to the other person now annoy the crap out of you. The differences that attracted you repel you. What started out as carefree and exciting is now predictable and boring. While dating, you saw the other person's best, but today all you see is their worst. The grass on everyone else's lawn seems so much greener. *Is it too late to unchoose?*

Going into marriage, my idea of love was words of affirmation, sex, touch, acts of kindness, sex, and more touch. What I've found, though, is that love in marriage often looks like grabbing a towel, getting down on the ground, and washing your spouse's dirty feet.

Washing your spouse's feet is speaking well of your spouse even when your friends are tearing down their husbands or wives—and your own spouse hurt your feelings the day before. It's seeing the best when the worst is quite obvious.

Love in marriage is listening to the other person share when you'd rather zone out. Doing laundry. Wiping kids' butts. Mowing the lawn. Putting the rug rats to bed when you're exhausted.

A key part of marriage (and any relationship) is giving love and not expecting to receive it in return. Not married? Don't have kids? You don't get to opt out of this! It applies to everyone. The closer you are to another person, the more you have to wash each other's feet. We are most like Jesus when we have towels around our waists.

This is the posture Becky has had since the day we got married. Groceries. Laundry. Shopping. Picking up the kids from school. Supporting me when it hasn't been easy. Forgiving me when I've let her down. Showing interest in the things I'm interested in only because she loves me.[5] Loving me when I say and do the wrong thing. Cheering me on. Keeping me humble when I think too highly of myself. Helping me stand when I feel inadequate.

Love is choosing to serve when you don't feel like it. Not keeping score. Not serving only if the other person serves you first. It's loving with no strings attached. Because loving with strings attached isn't love, and it soon becomes an obligation to the other person. Loving means serving day in, day out, not just on the special days, such as birthdays and anniversaries, but on the hard, normal, mundane days too.

Love is washing feet.

• • •

Bec and I have both been blessed with examples of what a great marriage looks like by our parents' marriages. The older we get, the more we realize our situation isn't the norm.[6] Bec's parents have been married for forty years and mine for forty-three. Thank you, God.

But over the past decade, the physical health of both of my parents has deteriorated. They're still not super old, and both were young when these issues started—specifically with my dad, who's had severe, life-altering pain for years. Most days he lays in bed for all but an hour or two. My parents have had to set aside dreams, slowing down much more than they would have liked.

My mom and dad are two peas in a pod, and someday they'll be lost without each other. My mom, though, has been a constant rock for my dad throughout his battle with pain. She serves him daily, helping him get dressed and take a shower and reminding him to take his meds. She speaks up for him at the doctor's office, at restaurants, and pretty much everywhere they go, making sure he's comfortable and has what he needs. She's his advocate. My mom's life looks completely different than she ever hoped, yet she does all this with a smile, constantly checking on my dad to make sure he's okay.

A few months back, my dad's pain flared to its worst yet. He couldn't move his hands. He couldn't even hold a phone. He couldn't do the most basic things, such as go to the bathroom by himself. The pain was so out of control that he went to the hospital to try to bring it to a manageable place. One of the hardest yet most beautiful moments to watch during this whole ordeal was my mom spoon-feeding my dad his meals because he couldn't do so himself. She did everything with patience, care, kindness, and love.

This is what true love looks like. Love washes feet.

Now, what does that really mean? Read on.

• • •

It was getting close to the time when Jesus would die on the cross. Jesus knew the time was coming, so he decided to share supper with those he was closest to—the twelve, his disciples. To be clear, Jesus had chosen to be around his twelve disciples. They were more than friends. He knew all their imperfections and shortcomings. He even knew which one would *betray* him. These guys had witnessed Jesus's love better than anyone. The way he treated people. The way he noticed people. The way he loved people. But Jesus had one last lesson to teach his disciples about love: how to serve.

During the meal, Jesus got up from the table, took off his outer clothing, and wrapped a towel around his waist. Then he poured water into a large bowl and began to wash his friends' feet.[7]

The disciples' feet would have been nasty. Not to mention Jesus was doing a job that was done only by servants and slaves, not rabbis or teachers. Why would Jesus dishonor himself like this? It was appalling! So much so that when Jesus bent down to wash Peter's feet, Peter protested, "You will never wash my feet!" Jesus replied that unless Peter allowed him to wash his feet, he wouldn't belong to Jesus. Peter quickly changed his tone after that, and with complete sincerity, he invited Jesus to wash all of him—his feet, his hands, everything.

After washing all the disciples' dirty, nasty feet (including the feet of Judas, the man who was about to betray Jesus—let *that* sink in!), Jesus stood up, put his coat back on, and started to explain what had just happened: "Do you understand what I have done? You look up to me as a teacher and Lord. As you should—I am both."

Jesus was telling them, "The best way I can explain how to become more like me, the best way I can explain what love truly looks like, is by getting down on my knees. It's by humbling myself in an action that is fit for a servant or slave, and it's in washing the dirtiest part of you. This is love. This is an example of what love looks like. This is what I, Jesus, have come to do, and if you want to look like me, do this for others."

It's like he's saying, "The people who don't deserve it? Wash *their* feet."

"The people who have hurt you—like my friend Judas here—wash their feet."

"If you think highly of yourself, wash the feet of others."

"Oh, you're a teacher? Someone who people look up to? Feet!"

If you've been a Christian for a long time, start washing feet.

What should you do for your spouse (if you have one) or any of the people closest to you who are often the hardest to love?

Pick up a towel.

Get scrubbing.

Feet.

• • •

This love cuts both ways. Sure, washing feet is humbling. But having your feet washed is a humbling experience too. Even saying the word *feet* makes me want to gag a little bit. It's like the word *moist* (shivers). The only thing worse that I can think of would be *moist feet*. (Okay, I'll stop!)

During my ordination service years ago, when I officially became an ordained pastor, a bishop washed my feet. It was a powerful moment. Unlike the disciples' feet though, my feet were clean. Spotless, actually. I made sure of it, knowing they would be seen by the bishop as well as by hundreds of people on a giant screen.

Want to spread love? Begin by washing feet. Get down on your knees, pull out a towel, and begin doing the things no one wants to do. Choose to do the jobs other people are avoiding. Do things for someone when no one else is watching. Voluntarily put the interests of the other person before your own. Look for ways to humble yourself while also lifting others up. Start washing feet! As I said before, even if you're not married, you're not exempt from this whole washing-feet thing. You have people in your life that you've chosen too. Your spouse or significant other, your friends, your roommate, your coworkers—look for ways to serve them!

I'll never forget a seminary professor friend of mine saying there's a part of God's heart that we'll never fully understand until we begin to serve others.[8] It's so true. There's a part of God we can't unlock, a part of Jesus's heart we'll never truly "get" until we experience what it's like to serve another human being.

Bec and I are now sixteen years into this thing called marriage. At times it feels like we're both on the same page; other times it feels like we're living in different universes. We wouldn't claim to have anything figured out or that we're qualified to write a book on how to have the perfect marriage. We both struggle to pick up a towel and wash feet, and just like every other human, we're self-centered, me-focused people. But each day, we decide to look at the example of Jesus.

Daily, Bec "washes my feet" in big and small ways.

Shaving the back of my neck when it gets hairy.[9]

Dropping off lunch at work when I've forgotten to bring something with me.

Reminding me of meetings that completely slipped my mind.

Speaking an encouraging word to me when I'm unsure that God can use me.

Choosing to love me each day, even when the warm, fuzzy feelings aren't there.

Giving an extra hand when I'm out in the garage doing who knows what and I can't do it on my own.

Sitting beside me after a day when I haven't been very patient or kind.

Each day, I do my best to get down on my knees and wash her feet too. Sixteen years in and so far it's just getting better and better each and every day.

Love washes feet.

PART 2

Some People I'm Learning to Love

Our job is to love others without stopping to inquire
whether or not they are worthy.

—Thomas Merton

11

Trevon

Love sees the person in front of you.

During the school year, Fridays are my favorite mornings of the week. They're one of my two days off, and for two-thirds of the day, it's just Bec and me, along with our youngest son, Anderson, instead of all four of our kids. I mean, I love all our kids, but sometimes it's nice to have some time with just my wife and one little gremlin (I say that in the most loving way possible).[1]

One winter Friday, after our kids had been dropped off at school, I was sitting in my living room and Bec was in the kitchen. All of a sudden I heard her yelling, "Stop! Stop for him! Stop!" She ran into the room I was in. "A boy just missed the school bus! He's running after it and waving, but the bus isn't stopping!" she explained.

"Right now?" I asked.

"Yes, he's still out there!"

I quickly ran outside in my socks. (Note: Did I mention it was winter? In South Dakota?)[2] The bus was already down the block, and I looked over to see a kid with his head down and backpack on, walking away from the bus stop.

"Hey! Hey!" I yelled in his direction. He turned around, almost like he thought he was in trouble. "Did you miss your bus?" He shrugged his shoulders.

"Do you have a way to get to school?" He shook his head no. His face said it all. He looked embarrassed and completely discouraged.

"Do you want a ride?"

Not expecting me to offer, the kid hesitated for a second and then said yes. I told him to meet me in the back alley by my garage. "I'll get my shoes on quickly, and I'll take you."

I walked back into the house and told my wife I was taking the kid to school. *Did I really just say that I was taking him? Should I actually take him? I kinda wanted to relax on my day off. Also, in this day and age, you have to worry about being accused of things. It does look a bit strange to see a grown man driving away with a random kid.* Feeling stuck because I had already said yes, I got my shoes on, went out to the garage, and opened the door for him.

When my garage door went up, he was standing there, waiting outside the door. The first thing out of his mouth was "You're my pastor!" He was grinning ear to ear.

"Really?" I said. "That's awesome! I guess that means we're family then. Hop in!"

Internally, I wondered, *How have I never seen this kid? Ever! On my block? In my own church? The church that I pastor!?* It bothered me that I hadn't noticed him before. Yet, sadly, I think we all have people in our lives like this. People that for whatever reason we just don't see, even if they're standing right in front of us.

"My school is a long way away," he warned me as we backed out of the garage.

Fifteen minutes later, I found he wasn't kidding—the school was half-way across town.[3] But I didn't mind—it gave us a chance to talk and get to know each other a little bit.

I learned that his name was Trevon and that he was a seventh grader living only a few blocks away from my house. Missing the bus wasn't a habit for Trevon; he'd only missed it twice this year.

I also found out which campus of my church he attended. Trevon went to church by himself, but he wasn't able to go very often. Most days he had to help his parents. His dad was sick, and his mom worked multiple jobs to provide for their family.

Even though Trevon was only a seventh grader, he had already experienced a lot more life than I had. That morning, he was standing on the side of the road, right in front of my house, and needed some help. Yeah, he needed a ride, but even more so, he needed encouragement. In the end, he did more for me on that ride to school than I could ever have done for him. He reminded me that the life situations we find ourselves in don't have to dictate our attitudes and our futures. He reminded me of the good in the world. He reminded me that love sees the person right in front of you.

The more Trevon talked and the more he told his story, I began to get the sense that he was a really good kid. I wanted him to hear it from me. I only hope that he heard a glimpse of God's grace and love through my words.

As a son and young man.

As a student.

As a part of my church.

"I am so proud of you," I said.

• • •

We often wonder how and where we can help people. *I want to do good,* many of us think, *but I don't know where to start.* Where is the need and how do we get there? Often Christians travel around the world to help others in need (which is awesome!), but we can miss the person right in front of us.

The person next door with cancer.

The coworker walking through a family conflict.

The old high school classmate struggling to make ends meet.

The family member or roommate dealing with discouragement or depression.

The seventh-grade neighbor you never knew you had.

Help them!

We don't always need to go somewhere else to help people; often we simply need to open our eyes to see the person in need right in front of us. The person who needs help right where we're at. Don't miss these people! These aren't the stories that make headlines or have thousands of retweets, but these moments—and more so, these people—matter.

• • •

At one point, an expert religious person approached Jesus and asked, "What does a person need to do to inherit eternal life?"[4] The religious guy didn't ask because he was curious. Instead he was asking the question to test Jesus, hoping to trip him up.

Now, depending on who you ask, you'll get a different answer to this man's question. Christians love to go back and forth on what the focus of our lives should be. What does a person need to do to make it into heaven? What should our priorities be for our time and attention? What's the most important thing when it comes to God? Often each person has a slightly different take on it.

Listen to what Jesus says, though: "Good question. Eternal life? Well, what does the Bible say?"

Knowing his Bible well, the religious man responded, " 'You must love the LORD your God with all your heart, all your soul, all your strength, and all your mind.' And, 'Love your neighbor as yourself.' "[5] Jesus agreed: "Yep, you're right! Now go do that and you will live."

Trying to show off how smart he was, the man asked Jesus a follow-up question: "And who is my neighbor?"

A little backstory here: At this time, Jewish law basically required Jewish people to help other Jewish people. If someone in their church (or, more accurately, their synagogue) needed help, they were required by religious law to help in any way they could. It was seen as a sin not to help a fellow Jew.[6]

Jesus answers in a way the man didn't expect—with a story. And it's an answer and story we're still talking about today. Listen in:

> A Jewish man was traveling from Jerusalem down to Jericho, and he was attacked by bandits. They stripped him of his clothes, beat him up, and left him half dead beside the road. By chance a priest came along. But when he saw the man lying there, he crossed to the other side of the road and passed him by. A Temple assistant walked over and looked at him lying there, but he also passed by on the other side. Then a despised Samaritan came along.

The priest and temple assistant were both people we expect to stop. It was a Jewish person lying on the side of the road all beaten up, and they were Jewish. Again, they were required to help! But neither of them stopped.

A Samaritan was a different story. For hundreds of years, there was a deep hatred between Jews and Samaritans. Jews basically saw Samaritans as half-breeds, a mixed group of people that weren't as pure or godly as they were.

The story continues:

> When [the Samaritan] saw the man, he felt compassion for him. Going over to him, the Samaritan soothed his wounds with olive oil and wine and bandaged them. Then he put the man on his own donkey and took him to an inn, where he took care of him. The next day he handed the innkeeper two silver coins, telling him, "Take care of this man. If his bill runs higher than this, I'll pay you the next time I'm here."

The proud religious leader listening to Jesus must have been speechless. He also was probably a bit appalled. The Samaritan, the person who was least expected to help, was the one who did in Jesus's story.

Then Jesus asked, "Now, which one of these three would you say was a neighbor to the man who was attacked by bandits?"

I can almost hear the man's sheepish reply, humbled and taken aback by Jesus's response to his arrogant question about who deserves to be loved. "The man replied, 'The one who showed him mercy.'"

Jesus leaves him with this: "Yes, now go and do the same."

The religious man expected an answer about heaven being open to those who followed all the rules, looked the part, and knew all the right talking points, as he did. Jesus said that's not the case. Heaven will be inherited by those who, out of a love for God, love their neighbors well, who bend down to help the people right in front of them.

· · ·

Now back to considering how and where we can help people.

Step one? Slow down.

When you're running through each day at a thousand miles per hour, it's hard to notice the people along the road of your life. Take your eyes off your phone and look up. Instead of cramming another thing in between meetings, breathe and say hello to the person next to you.

Step two? Keep your eyes open.

Who's the person right in front of you, the person God placed in your life whom he's hoping you don't miss? I had no idea Trevon was my neighbor or that he even went to my church. He was there the whole time, right in front of me, and I was too busy looking around at other things to realize he needed help.

Who's that person for you? Who's your neighbor? Who's your Trevon?

Maybe there's a friend you haven't talked to in a while who you're too scared to reach out to. Maybe you know your coworker has been going through a rough time, but you don't know how to help. Maybe it's your mom. Maybe it's your brother. Maybe it's literally your next-door neighbor. All these people, they're your neighbors. Love them! Love the people you see.

Through the story of the good Samaritan, Jesus teaches us that love isn't always flashy or showy. We don't have to travel thousands of miles or be recognized for our good deeds to love well. Instead we just need to see people. To notice them. To realize when they're in need and go out and love them.

Maybe that's buying someone coffee and really listening to what they have to say. Maybe it's smiling at your coworker or helping her pack up and move across town. Maybe it's helping someone fill out a job application. Helping your friend set up a personal budget. Helping someone get his car fixed. Maybe it's taking in a single mom and her kids until she's able to get back on her feet. Maybe it's giving a kid on your block a ride to school.

Whatever this looks like in your life, we can be sure of this: love sees the person right in front of us. How do we know this? Because Jesus himself showed us how to love like this. He was the master of seeing those that others drove—or walked—right past.

• • •

I'm so glad that I had the chance to drive Trevon to school that day. Trust me, I'm far from an expert on loving people like Jesus does, but that day I learned that when we see those around us, we benefit at least as much as they do. Trevon got a ride to school that day and kind words from his pastor—but he inspired me! He reminded me of the incredible stories that surround us all the time and how many times I walk past opportunities because I'm too busy, too consumed with other things, too focused on my agenda for the day.

As I pulled up to Trevon's school, I told him how proud I was to be his pastor. And now I was his friend.

As he got out of the car, I said, "Well, now you know where we live, and again, we're family, so stop by if you ever want to talk or need help with anything. I'd do anything for you."

12

Tony

Love reaches out to the different.

One of the volunteers who used to run the cameras on Sunday mornings at Embrace would sometimes show up with a trace of remaining makeup under his eyes from the night before. *His* eyes, not hers. His name? Tony.

Why was there makeup on this dude? Well, a lot of Saturday nights, Tony dresses up as a drag entertainer.[1]

Quick confession: One time in college I pulled an all-nighter while sitting at a restaurant called Fryn' Pan, studying for an economics test the next day.[2] While I was in the restroom, a six-foot, eight-inch guy dressed in drag walked in. The guy didn't say a word to me, but for some reason I was scared, like seeing-a-big-guy-down-a-dark-alley kind of scared. I'm not sure if it was his height or the fact that I was just a small-town kid who had never seen a drag queen before, but I had a nightmare about it later that week.

We're often scared of things that are different, aren't we?

But different doesn't necessarily mean bad or wrong. It simply means not like us.

Good or bad. Right or wrong.

Someone who's physically different from us or has a disability. Someone who's passionate about something we know nothing about. Someone who thinks differently and lives differently. Different politics, morals, whatever.

It takes us aback.

But back to Tony. He had started coming to the church a few years ago after another church had made it fairly clear he wasn't welcome. He was a recovering alcoholic who was broken and hurting. Having grown up in a traditional church where he knew all the right answers but didn't totally fit in, Tony wondered if there was still a place for him in church.

Each week, I saw Tony faithfully and skillfully serving—showing up to volunteer before most churchgoers were even awake. In the past, Tony had helped with sound and tech on different Christian music tours and at churches, but more than being good at moving switches, Tony was quick to love on people. Often, he'd show up in the morning with a pastor's or other volunteer's favorite coffee drink, expecting nothing in return.

Tony, who always walked in with a positive attitude.

Tony, who was willing to do anything.

Tony, who was part of our family.

On a regular basis, Tony told me just how thankful he was for his church family. But really, I was so thankful that Tony was part of our family. He might have been in drag on Saturdays, but at our church Tony was just Tony.

Over the years, Tony and I talked about God's plan for our lives, including sexuality, candidly sharing where he and I agreed and disagreed. But what was never a question? Tony's love for me and my love for Tony. Even more so than that, God's love for the both of us.

Something I'll never forget was Tony's sobriety birthday. It was a Sunday, and Tony showed up to volunteer at church, bringing a big cookie cake. Between services, he let me know that he had left a piece of the cake back in my room. Mesmerized by the thought of cookie cake, I quickly left our conversation to devour every ounce of the piece he had left me. It was seriously amazing. Afterward, I went searching for Tony to thank him. I found him at the front of the church as people were coming in for the next service.

"How's your birthday been so far?" I asked.

"Honestly, it's been really hard," he said. "Recently I told my parents that I'm bisexual. They invited me to lunch, and I had no idea what to expect. My dad said they didn't approve of my lifestyle and went on to say I'm the biggest disappointment in the history of our family."

I stood and listened as he emotionally shared. After a few moments, I spoke. "Well, Tony, that sucks! And I'm sorry your dad said that. I'm sure he's processing a lot of things himself. But just know that you're not a disappointment. You're not a disappointment to me. You're not a disappointment to our church. We wouldn't be the same church without you."

Just because we're different doesn't mean we're disappointments.

Later that day, in the midst of the drag pictures on his Instagram, Tony posted a picture of the view from behind the camera at church where he had served that morning. His caption?

"I celebrated my birthday today with my favorite family. I love this church."

• • •

In the Bible, we're introduced to a group of people called lepers. Different from sinners—people who were known for doing bad things—lepers were simply seen as unclean, not because of what they did but because of who they were.

You might know that leprosy is a disease that affects the skin. As it progresses, pain turns to numbness and the skin loses its original color, becoming thick, glossy, and scaly. Sores and ulcers develop around the eyes and ears, and the skin begins to bunch up. Leprosy also affects the sufferer's voice and ability to speak.

Much worse than the physical aspect of leprosy, though, is how it used to impact people socially. Back in Bible times, lepers were required to shout, "Unclean!" as they approached a crowd, to make sure no one accidentally touched them. Talk about something that could immediately make you feel less than human.

On one occasion, Jesus crossed paths with a leper.[3] The leper noticed Jesus, and even though the leper knew it was against the rules, he approached him.

Jesus had the ability to heal his leprosy, but would he want to do the unthinkable? Would he want to reach out and *touch* this unclean man? Would he heal him by staying an arm's length away? At the risk of catching the physical disease and becoming spiritually unclean, Jesus reached out and touched the leper. Yes, he did want to touch him. Jesus reached out and healed the leper.

In that moment, a man who hadn't been touched in years was touched. He was touched by the one who was able to heal him from the inside out. He was touched by Jesus. Skin to skin. It's reported that human beings need eight to ten touches each day to remain physically and emotionally healthy. Can you imagine having not been touched by anyone in years?

• • •

Touch matters.[4]

When I was growing up, it was always a big deal when Dad reached out to hold my hand and it disappeared into his. Nothing was better than stepping off the school bus and getting a hug from Mom. Or a pat on the back from my high school football coach after a game. A high five from a buddy. A touch on the shoulder from someone thanking me for impacting his life. When I met my wife, I'll never forget the first time we touched hands.[5] And last night when I went to the hospital to pray with an eighty-four-year-old man from my church, he reached out and held my hand during the prayer.[6]

Touch binds two people together. Touch unites.[7] When we touch, we literally cross into another person's space. The two become one in marriage, but on a small level, this happens each time we touch someone. We communicate, *You are worthy of love. You are made in the image of God. You are lovely. You are beautiful.*

Being touched matters.[8]

How amazing would it be to be physically touched by Jesus?

• • •

People like Tony are often considered lepers in most churches. The church doesn't go so far as to say they shouldn't be there, and people aren't required to shout, "Unclean!" as they walk through the doors, but we're careful not to get too close. To touch them. To associate with them. To love them well.

Even if it's never addressed from the stage, a lot of churches have made it crystal clear that some kinds of people are welcome and some kinds are not. It's not just that what they're doing is wrong, it's who they are that's wrong.

Whether it's a person's sexuality.

Or she has had an affair.

Or he got a DUI.

She has committed a crime.

His son is struggling with drugs.

Her daughter got pregnant when it wasn't planned.

We draw our line in the sand, and if a person even gets near that line, then that person really shouldn't be coming through the doors on Sundays. We say . . .

"It's not that you can't come; we just don't really want you here."

"It's not that you're not invited; it's just that you don't really fit in."

"It's not that we don't love you as a Christian should; it's just that we don't approve of what you're doing and we want you to know that."

Sound familiar? Maybe you've been in a church like this before. Maybe you've even been this person before. A friend recently told me, "If you're different in any way, the church is the last place you want to be. The church sees a unicorn and says, 'Not good!'"[9]

But what if the church welcomed and loved unicorns—people who are different—better than any other group, organization, or movement the world had to offer? Other groups *appear* to welcome people, but if you look past the surface, they typically only welcome people who are like them, think like them, vote like them, live like them. What if the church was different?

I can only hope that my church, other churches, and the worldwide church would look like the church Jesus had in mind. I want to pastor a church full of people who look like the people Jesus hung out with. The people no one else wanted to touch with a ten-foot pole but whom Jesus came close to. Because really, we're all lepers in some way. There's a lot of unclean stuff in our lives; it's just harder to see our own leprosy than it is to see the leprosy of others.

Want to love people who are different from you? Get uncomfortable. Have actual conversations with people you know think differently from you. Move from your space to someone else's. Meet others on their ground. In *their* place of comfort, not yours. Ask questions. Ask them to share their stories and then listen. Agree to disagree.[10]

If there's one thing we've lost as a society, it's the ability to think differently and still love and respect each other. We like to polarize and pigeonhole people. Conservatives polarize progressives. Progressives polarize conservatives. Sad! If people are different from us, we like to label and demonize. It's impossible to love someone we've labeled.

But love breaks rules. Love sets aside fear. Love reaches beyond those who are like us.

Just like me, Tony isn't a perfect person. As his pastor, it wasn't my job to change him, or anyone—that's God's job. As it is with any other person in my church, my job was to come near to Tony. To tell him about God's grace and truth. To love him well and ultimately point him to Jesus. Jesus is the one who will turn his life upside down, as Jesus continues to do with mine.

I want my love to look like Jesus healing the leper. Ironically, Tony did this better for me than I ever did for him. Tony's love reaches beyond those who are like him, even to a pastor who once had a nightmare about a drag queen. That's how I want my love to look. Needless to say, I'm still a work in progress.

● ● ●

A few months back, Tony took a promotion that moved him out of town. But before leaving, he shared on Facebook about his love for the church and the different people in it. He tagged me.

I have to admit, my first thought was, *Do I remove the tag? What will other pastors and Christians think of me being tagged by a guy whose Facebook page is full of drag pictures?* I love Tony so much, but I worried that I would receive negative emails and scrutiny during a season when I already had thin skin and didn't want any more haters. Would being publicly associated with Tony make me "unclean" in the eyes of others? Sad, right?

After going back and forth in my head for a while, I felt Jesus speak: *If you want to associate with the people I associate with, you might want to hang out with more people like Tony, not less. He's my son. Dearly loved. And, Adam, I've associated with you for your entire life, and I know your own uncleanness just as much as Tony's.*

Mic drop! Looking back, I'm embarrassed that I even hesitated. Tony, I'm sorry.

Months have passed since Tony moved, but about a week ago, he came back to town for the closing of his house. The first place he stopped? The church. Tony and I talked for a couple of hours. Laughing. Catching up. He shared about the transition and his search for a new church home and AA group. I can't put into words how much I needed the time spent with Tony.

Before leaving, he hugged me. *Touch.* I needed a hug.

Over the thirteen years of being a pastor, I've had quite a few followers of Jesus walk out of my life. People who knew the Bible well but walked away for no specific reason. Then there are people like Tony who, even after he moved hours away, still didn't leave me. He stayed. He reached out to see how I was doing. He cared for me. He loved me.

It's strange how sometimes a leper can look more like Jesus than the religious person. Love reaches out and touches those who are considered unclean.

Love reaches out to the person who is different. Period.

13

Mark

Love faces the two-faced.

There's no one I struggle to love more than Pharisees. No one.

These are the people who enjoy pointing out the shortcomings of others. People who think they are holier and better than the next person because of their (insert sarcastic tone here) deep insights, religious perfection, spiritual intensity, and eloquent words. It's almost like they've never read the words of Jesus they so boldly and proudly proclaim as true.

In Jesus's day, Pharisees were the elite religious leaders. The people who looked super pious and saw themselves as experts of the Law. Like church "good ole boys" who have been there forever—and not in a good way. It almost seemed like they owned the place.

The Pharisees proudly claimed to know what was right and what was wrong better than anyone. And it was *all* about rules. This group of people viewed it as their job—on behalf of God, of course—to point out the shortcomings, errors, and sin in the lives of everyone around them. At the same time, they failed to look at the sin in their own lives.

We may not use the term *Pharisee* today, but they're still with us.[1] To some degree, there's a Pharisee inside each of us (there's definitely one inside me). In a few areas of our lives or maybe all areas, we think we have it all figured out. That our ways are best. That we have it all together. Even when it comes to God, some of us think we have all the answers, that we're better than the next person.

But the truth is, we're not. And even *thinking* we're better makes us worse than the person with the more visible sin. Ironically enough, the Pharisees' lives were often the very opposite of the heart of Jesus. Jesus used his strongest words to deal with these religious people. I think we "church people" are quick to forget that!

• • •

A few years ago, a guy named Mark started attending Embrace. After his first service with us, Mark quickly sought me out after worship, sharing a few things he really liked about the church. I said, "Wonderful. Thank God!"

He then went on to say, "But one thing I wanted to mention to you . . . I wish you would dig deeper into the Word. I always like it when the pastor shares what different words mean in the Greek and really moves past the surface. The message is good, but I want to go deeper in my walk with Jesus. I think if you did this it would really help get me there."

I told him about a few places where he could dig deeper into the verses and the book of the Bible I had shared from that morning. Mark didn't really seem all that interested in finding out more that way, but he thanked me for talking with him and left.

Next Sunday, Mark found me after the service once again. This time he mentioned one or two things he liked from the service and then quickly asked, "Does the church have any groups that really dig deeper? I've been following Jesus a long time and want to go past the surface. Everything you shared is great for new people, but I've heard most of it before."

I mentioned a couple groups that were going through a book of the Bible in detail, but when Mark found out I wasn't personally leading the groups, he didn't seem interested. So, I encouraged him to consider leading a group himself. Especially with his knowledge of the Bible, I assumed he'd jump at the chance to pour into others. Mark quickly shared that his life was quite busy, his kids were involved in a lot of sports, and he didn't really have time to add another thing.

"No problem. Just an idea," I said.

Over the course of the next few weeks, Mark sought me out each and every Sunday to share his thoughts on the service. Instead of starting the conversation by saying what he had liked, though, he only shared what he thought was missing—not just from the service itself, but from other areas of the church as well.

"The church should have more volunteers," he said, but he wasn't able to join a serving team himself. He wanted to see our finances—which we post on our website—but he admitted he wasn't currently giving.

With each week that passed, I could see Mark's frustration with the church growing and growing. Typically, when we think of "consumer churches," we think of churches that try to entertain crowds with flashy lights, set pieces, and musicians, hoping to attract people. People who are "shallow church consumers" hop from church to church, just wanting to be entertained and feel good.

But there's a subtler version of church consumers who, on the outside, appear much more holy. The "deep church consumer" isn't looking to do anything for the church or actually serve, but they're vocal about the church being exactly how they like it and nothing else.

I want to be fed. Why doesn't the church do more of this? Does the church care about that? I'm not feeling personally convicted. Why can't I meet with the pastor on a regular basis? Mark reminded me of this type of person.

It doesn't really matter if you're a "shallow" Christian or a "deep" Christian; you can still be a consumer. Yes, we should all be asking ourselves if we're learning and growing at a certain church. But honestly, the church isn't there to serve our needs. Speaking of Greek words, the early church was described using the word *koinonia,* which means "a community that contributes." What would happen if we judged our level of "deep" by what we contributed rather than by what we were fed?

As a healthy thirty-eight-year-old guy, I can't imagine asking my dad to feed me. Even though he's the nicest person I know, he'd probably kindly respond by saying, "What? Are you joking? Can't you feed yourself, Adam?"

This is what we're doing when we, as adult Christians, ask for the church to feed us. It's not the church's job to do that—it's our job! Are you connected to a group? Are you giving? Serving? Digging into the message and Bible on your own time? That's how you get fed spiritually by a church, not by showing up once a week and expecting thirty minutes of a pastor speaking from the stage to carry you through the ups and downs of your week.

But back to our story. A few weeks passed, and Mark no longer sought me out on Sundays. I figured he had gone looking for a new church.[2] If I'm being honest, in years past I would have tried to convince people like Mark to stay, but in this moment I found myself simply feeling thankful that he had moved on. I love that different churches have specific focuses and passions that reach and minister to people in different places in their relationship with Jesus. Jesus called the church the body of Christ. Some churches are the hands, and others are the feet.[3] I hoped Mark had found a church that filled him up in ways that Embrace could not.

I hadn't thought about Mark in a while until one day when I got an email from him that said he needed to meet with me. He explained he had talked with two other people who shared similar concerns about the church, and they wanted to ask me some questions. I replied that I would love to connect, and we set a date.

I didn't think much more about the email until I walked into a room with Mark and the two other concerned people a few weeks later. Even before a word was spoken, I knew we weren't about to have a friendly meeting chatting about Jesus. I sat down and immediately the questions began.

"We need more theology on Sundays. More meat. More substance. I want to really press in and worship. What is the church doing to bring people deeper?"

"Your church is based on the story of the prodigal son? That's a nice story, but it's not a good basis for a church. Actually, it's pretty unbiblical. Have you ever considered changing Embrace's name?"

"I love that we welcome first-time guests, but church on Sundays isn't for them. It's for people who already follow Jesus, not unbelievers. Sundays should only be for the people who are already Christians. Can you change this?"

I again brought up different places where they could serve. I talked about them leading a group to "go deeper" in the specific ways they had mentioned. I shared the heart and story of Embrace's biblical basis. But it was clear these weren't the answers Mark and the two others were looking for. A couple weeks passed after our meeting, and I expected them to tell me that Embrace wasn't the right church for them and that they'd leave to find a different church that would better fit their wants. Instead, I got a phone call from a friend.

"Adam, a guy named Mark reached out to me. I don't know who he is, but he said he's concerned about the church. He's been sharing all kinds of things with me and a few others that just aren't true."

It turns out Mark and his friends had left the church, but instead of talking more to me about their issues, they had talked to anyone who would listen. I was heartsick.

I wanted to body-slam Mark! I wanted to say to him, "What does God have to say about gossip? What about trying to hurt and divide a church? What about spreading things that are untrue? You want to go deeper, but you've never led a small group yourself? You want to go deeper, but you have no time to serve? You love pointing out the faults of others, but I've never heard you say anything about your own shortcomings. You want to go deeper, but all I'm hearing from you is 'me, me, me, me.'"

Time and time again, Jesus called out the religious leaders of his day. When I say "called out," I mean he used his strongest words against them: Vipers. Hypocrites. Cups that are clean on the outside but ugly on the inside. People he knows from afar.[4]

I was so mad at these vipers and wanted to point out all the places where they were wrong. As I was throat-punching people in my head, I opened up Twitter, only to see this tweet from Scott Sauls:

"The 'Grace Pharisee' is judgmental toward judgmental people, an unloving Pharisee toward unloving Pharisees."[5]

An "unloving Pharisee toward unloving Pharisees." Ouch!

I was unknowingly turning into a Grace Pharisee while dealing with these Pharisees in my life. By calling out the lack of grace these Pharisees extended to others, I was becoming one too. It was a hard pill for me to swallow. The difference between Jesus and me is that though Jesus calls out the Pharisees, he still loves them unconditionally. I just wanted to call them out. No love!

I probably struggle with loving Pharisees because even though I know a lot about Jesus, I know I have nothing figured out. I've been following Jesus for more than twenty years, have a master of divinity degree, and have been an ordained pastor for more than a decade, yet it seems that I know very little besides the fact that I'm a recovering sinner in need of Jesus.[6] I fail constantly. The last thing I would ever want to do is proudly point out the shortcomings in everyone else's life.

Being even more honest, I struggle to love Pharisees because I care deeply about what other people think of me, and I don't want them pointing out what they view as shortcomings in me personally, in my relationship with Jesus, or in the church I pastor.

It's also a lot easier to recognize the Pharisee in others than it is in yourself. We do that with a lot of things, don't we? It's easy to see the error in other people's lives. It's easier to see the mistakes, pride, and jealousy in others than it is in ourselves.

I immediately put up a wall in my heart when faced with the arrogant attitude of a Pharisee. I get defensive. And when that happens—*just like a Pharisee*—I stop caring about the person in front of me. In these moments, I could honestly care less about his story, who he is, or loving him.

Maybe he genuinely wants to grow in his love and understanding of God. Maybe she's struggling with an addiction and trying to hide it behind a righteous cover. Maybe he grew up in a strict home where he only heard about God's wrath, never about his love. Maybe she believes the lie that you can somehow earn God's grace and she's never felt worthy of his attention.

When the walls are up in our hearts, we don't have the ability to think or love clearly. So how exactly do we love the Pharisees in our lives without becoming Grace Pharisees?

I think Jesus has some answers for us.

• • •

At one point in the Bible, we meet a Pharisee named Nicodemus who sought out Jesus.[7] Nicodemus came to Jesus one evening, confused, so he asked Jesus a follow-up question: "How can an old man go back into his mother's womb and be born again?"

Jesus responded and told Nicodemus about the Holy Spirit and how God makes us new. But once again Nicodemus asked Jesus a question: "How are these things possible?"

Jesus was direct with him and spoke candidly: "You are a respected Jewish teacher, and yet you don't understand these things?"

Translation: *If you're a good religious person, how can you possibly not know this?*

Yet Jesus went on to share about how "God so loved the world" and everyone in it that "he gave His only son" so that anyone, literally *any* person who believed in him, would "have eternal life."

Jesus didn't beat around the bush with Nicodemus. Instead he called him out. Gently. Speaking truth, though with grace and love.

"How can you not know this?" quickly changed to "Let me tell you about how much God loves you." Grace and truth. That's once again how Jesus loves.

A year or so later, Nicodemus crossed paths with Jesus again. This time, though, it wasn't so he could ask Jesus more questions. Jesus had just died on the cross, and his body was about to be laid in a grave. Nicodemus showed up to help prepare Jesus's body to be buried. We're told that Nicodemus brought about seventy-five pounds of myrrh, aloes, and some other essential oils to help with the burial.[8]

Nicodemus's life had been changed by Jesus. After Jesus was crucified, all the crowds and even Jesus's followers scattered. Nicodemus (and as we mentioned earlier, Joseph of Arimathea) never left Jesus's side. Nicodemus—this imperfect Pharisee—was there.

Jesus loved Nicodemus by speaking grace and truth. In what specific ways?

Truth: Jesus realized the gap between Nicodemus's heart and his head. He knew Nicodemus needed to get his heart in line with his knowledge about God.

Grace: Obviously Jesus let Nicodemus keep hanging out with him. He didn't reject him. Jesus kept teaching Nicodemus about the ways God loved him. Jesus loved Nicodemus so fully that Nicodemus was one of the only ones with Jesus at the end, never leaving his side.

How does that translate to us? Instead of writing people off, help them understand. We can't just get mad at the Pharisees in our lives; we need to help them move their head knowledge into their hearts. We should never start by shutting people out of our lives. It's so easy to run away from a Pharisee, but instead let's keep pursuing them, just like Jesus does.[9]

That's how we should love Pharisees. Not by calling them out and becoming Pharisees ourselves, but by lovingly facing the two-faced. It's convicting for me even as I write this.

. . .

Who is it that you struggle to love? Maybe, like me, Pharisees are at the top of your list. Or maybe there's another group of people, a specific person, or a personality trait that's hard for you to love. Whatever it is, I would tell you to follow the model Jesus set out for us in the story of Nicodemus. Don't stoop to their level and do the very thing that you hate. Speak truth, but also extend love.[10]

I know myself, and I know the tendency I have to be a Grace Pharisee. But I'm realizing the hard truth that me hating a Pharisee is just as bad as someone else hating a sinner. Truly loving the Pharisees in my life is something I'm working on every day. They're people too. People who God loves and wants to be in relationship with.

The good news is, Jesus can change the heart of anyone: the Pharisee, the sinner, and even me. Even you. Let's model a love that extends to the Pharisees in our lives—a love Jesus showed Nicodemus, a love that faces the two-faced in our lives and shows them the grace and truth Jesus so perfectly shows to us.

14

Captain

Love doesn't always look like love.

Last year on my way home from our Sunday evening church service, I saw a man lying on his back in the middle of the road.

A block from my house.

At 8 p.m.

Pitch black.

Eight degrees outside.

On a random side street that few drive on.

Knowing I might be the only person who would see him, I reluctantly pulled my car over. I was exhausted from preaching all day, it was cold, and I just wanted to go home. But instead, I got out and walked up to him. I quickly realized he was okay, just drunk. I say "just drunk" because, unfortunately, running into intoxicated people lying on the ground is a fairly regular thing in my neighborhood. The man had to be around the same age as my dad, and even though it's fairly normal to meet people like him in our part of town, it still bothers me every time.

This guy could be someone's dad, and here he was, lying drunk in the middle of the road. I wasn't embarrassed for him—embarrassed is something you feel when someone makes a mistake. Instead, I was heartsick, realizing the state he was in was probably pretty normal for him.

I approached the man, who was still lying on his back, and asked how he was doing.

He quickly responded, "Fantastic! Can you help me up?"

Yeah, rewind. I *wish* that's what he'd said. Instead, he greeted me with a different kind of f-word, one with four letters.

"I'm fine! Leave me the f— alone!" he snapped.

I replied, "Well, you don't look fine. And I can't leave you alone because you might freeze to death."

He snapped back again: "Leave me the f— alone. Get out of here."

Instead of arguing, I asked him his name.

"What?"

"What's your name?"

He mumbled a bit and then said, "Captain."

I wasn't sure if he was giving me the name of his favorite drink (Captain Morgan Rum) or his actual name, but I went with it.

"Well, Captain, we need to get you up off the ground and to someplace warm."

He cursed under his breath. I pulled him up, got him on his feet, and started walking with him toward my car. We made it a few steps before I turned around, only to see him stumble and fall into a snowbank along the side of the road. This time he was almost completely covered in snow.

"Leave me the f— alone! I'll be fine. I don't want to be touched."

Snowbanks in South Dakota can grow into small mountains (and did I mention it was only eight degrees outside?). Even though I really didn't want to touch him or help in any way for that matter (truthfully, I just wanted to walk away at this point), I knew that I couldn't, especially since he was now nearly buried in snow. Instead, I got Captain into a sitting position, while he called me every name under the sun. I sat and began to talk with him. I told him that God loves him. And because I knew that no homeless shelter would take him in his drunken state, I did the most loving thing I could do at that point: without him knowing, I called the cops. They'd take him in for the night until he sobered up.

It would have been easy to just drive past him, to walk away after he had said those unkind things and asked me to leave, instead of sitting with him. But he needed to be loved, even if he didn't want to be loved. Sometimes love means calling the cops. Sometimes love doesn't always look like love.

I waited till the cops showed up. Captain's stream of choice words quickly moved from me to them. I watched as they treated him with kindness and helped him when he asked them not to. I told him to have a good night as he muttered under his breath at the cops. At least for the night, they kept him from freezing.

In thinking about this more than once since then, here's what has struck me: there are quite a few people like Captain in our lives. People who don't want help, or at least don't want to admit they do. People who choose to stay where they are (even if the place they're in is terrible), rather than making a hard change that's needed. People who push you away when you reach out. People you love who continue to make poor decision after poor decision. People who call you unkind things when you ask for their names while they're lying in the middle of the road.

People who need love but don't want it.

· · ·

Jesus knew one of these people. His name was Legion. A guy named Mark shared the story with us.[1]

Something to know about this story is that, aside from the main heroes of the Bible, we're not usually given a lot of detail about the people Jesus met. We're briefly introduced to a person, Jesus does something awesome, and then we move on to the next character.

This isn't true with Legion. Instead, he's elaborately described. He's a man possessed by evil demons. He lives in terrible conditions, places such as burial caves and tombs. He's well known by everyone who lives in the area. He's a violent man who, even with chains, can't be restrained.

Because Legion was uncontrollable, the people in the nearby town had driven him out into the country, where he wandered the caves and hills, howling and cutting himself.[2]

Doesn't really sound like someone you would want to meet in a dark alley, does it?

When Legion saw Jesus, Legion ran up to him, and the demons inside him immediately yelled, "What do you want? What do you want from me? Leave me alone!" (The demons are speaking for Legion here, not the man himself—kind of creepy if you ask me.) But Jesus didn't listen!

Jesus didn't leave when Legion yelled at him to stay away. Jesus didn't walk past Legion. He didn't ignore him. Instead, *Jesus asked Legion his name.*

"My name is Legion," he replied, "for we are many."

After hearing Legion's name, Jesus commanded the demons to leave this man, sending them off to enter a group of nearby pigs (yep, you read that right, pigs). Craziest story ever!

Even crazier, after the demons went out, Legion begged Jesus to stay, instead of pushing him away. He didn't want to leave Jesus's side. Don't miss this: Legion wanted to stay near the one person who didn't listen to him when he said he didn't want to be loved. The demons controlling him were the ones wanting to push Jesus away, refusing to accept his love, but once this man was himself again, all he wanted was to be close to the love Jesus was offering.

Now, maybe we haven't experienced a lot of demon possession in our day (besides watching *The Exorcist*), but I'd argue we all have "demons" in our lives that tell us to stay isolated, to stay disconnected from the love of other people even when we know it's not what's best for us. These demons take a lot of different shapes, but many are all too familiar to us: shame, voices of self-doubt, hidden pain, fear, lust, jealousy, bitterness, addiction—the list could go on forever. These not-so-hidden demons inside each of us tell us we don't deserve to be loved.

Jesus had enough love for Legion to ignore his yelling and go a step further and heal him. Afterward, this healed man craved Jesus's presence, his friendship. He's filled with gratitude because Jesus saw him, loved him, and made him whole. Legion is changed, and we can be too.

• • •

Legion's story and Captain's story teach us that sometimes we need to get closer, even when people push us away. I've found that people, including myself, often push others away because of the demons mentioned above: shame, fear, pride, and so on.

We're ashamed. We need help, but we're embarrassed to let another person in. We're in a dark place, but we worry what others will think if we let them in on our secrets.

We're fearful. We're afraid others will see us at our worst and want nothing to do with us. We're scared that, even if we do seek help, no one will be brave enough to sit with us in our pain. We'll be more alone than ever.

We're prideful. We convince ourselves that we don't need someone else to help us out of the mess we're in, even though we know we're drowning. We have a reputation to keep, so people can't know we deal with this kind of stuff. We have to pull ourselves up. We're better than that.

Like Legion, our inner demons often convince us that we're too far gone. All hope is lost. That we need to stay away from others. We've just decided this is who we are and how we're always going to be. We feel unlovable. Like we can't be helped. Like we were meant to be alone.

Now, we know this can happen to us, but it's also true of others. Sometimes when people say "stay away," they actually mean "please help me. Come closer. I'm scared."[3]

It can be hard to distinguish between the two—some people *actually* want you to stay away (can I get an amen from introverts worldwide?).[4] But others are just too scared or ashamed or stuck to ask for help when they need it. Just think back to yourself. More often than not, we want help and we need help, but we just don't know how to ask for it. Again, we're ashamed. Fearful. Prideful.

But instead of walking away from us, Jesus gets closer. He encourages us to do the same for others. What does this look like?

For you, it might be challenging a friend who's making poor decisions. This can be really hard to do, especially if other "friends" are the ones leading him to make those poor decisions.

It might mean telling your mom who struggles with addiction that she can't live with you but that the moment she's ready to get help, you'll be the first person there.

It might mean encouraging a friend that she can do better than the guy she's currently dating, knowing that she so badly wants to be in a relationship that she's just not seeing (or she's ignoring) all the warning signs that keep coming up.

It might mean not giving any more money to your kid who's just spending it on drugs and alcohol—allowing him to truly hit rock bottom instead of bailing him out time and time again.

It might mean speaking the hard truth to someone even when she doesn't want to hear it. Telling someone, "You hurt me. That hurt. It's not okay."[5]

• • •

Sometimes love might even mean taking your daughter to rehab.

When I was eight, my parents adopted my sister, Becca, from South Korea as a two-year-old.[6] I can't remember a time when she wasn't part of our family. Given that I was the closest in age to her, she and I quickly became friends (and also enemies at times).

As she got older, even though she knew she was a part of our family, Becca began to notice the differences between her and the rest of our family—skin color and eye shape, among other things.

When we were growing up, our home was the most loving, stable home I can imagine. My parents showered us daily with love, both in words and actions. They loved my sister not *like* one of their own but *as* their own. Still, my sister had questions and wrestled with her identity and where she fit in.

In high school, Becca started struggling with alcohol. She couldn't always handle or process some things well, and drinking became an escape. By the time she was a freshman in college, her drinking was no longer just a concern; it was a problem that was impacting every part of her life. She got into trouble with the law and was kicked out of school after only one semester. What would she do next? My parents made the decision for her: they took her to rehab.

Mom and Dad made the two-and-a-half-hour drive from Watertown, South Dakota, to Fargo, North Dakota, to pick her up, along with all her belongings. They then drove four and a half hours to the Keystone Treatment Center in Canton, South Dakota.

After thirty days in the facility, my sister would never touch alcohol again. Now twelve years sober, she's married, a wonderful mom of two, and I'm so proud to be her brother, as I always have been. What sticks out to me the most about her story? Years after treatment, my sister randomly mentioned one day that the moment she knew Mom and Dad loved her was the day they brought her to rehab.

"What?" I said. "It wasn't the *years* of them caring for you, expressing their love, or giving you attention?"

"No, it was the day they brought me to Keystone. I knew they must really love me to do something like that."[7]

Unlike my sister's story, Captain's story doesn't have a pretty ending, at least that I'm aware of. The cops came and picked him up. The truth is, I don't know the end of Captain's story. But God does. And as long as Captain is alive and kicking, God isn't done with him yet. My prayer is that once Captain sobered up, he remembered that someone cared enough about him to pull over and offer him help. I hope others came alongside Captain as well. If he was truly wanting to change, I pray that someone would be there to help him take the first step. We can't do this thing called life alone, especially when trying to overcome an addiction.

The results are up to God, not us. We do our part, and God does his.

Love doesn't always look warm and fuzzy.[8] It isn't always nice. It doesn't always say what you want to hear. Sometimes it gives you the hard truth.

Sometimes love looks like calling the cops.

Like staying when you're asked to leave.

Like sending your daughter to rehab.

Sometimes love doesn't look like love. At least not at first. Instead it looks like Jesus's interaction with Legion—staying when he was being asked to keep his distance. It's calling someone out on the harmful things that are happening in his life, knowing that a negative reaction doesn't necessarily mean that person doesn't want to be loved. It's knowing what's best for someone even if he (or the demons inside him) doesn't want to hear it.

Sometimes love looks like Jesus and Legion. It doesn't always look like love.

15

Shirley

Love notices the unnoticeable.

Recently I was in the midst of a busy travel season, speaking at different conferences and churches. It's always humbling and exciting to share in front of larger crowds, but it can also be incredibly lonely. You're away from your family, and once the line of people asking to talk with you disappears, often you end up sitting in a coffee shop or hotel room by yourself. There's only so much *Fixer Upper* you can watch!

To someone wired like my more introverted wife, this might seem like a dream (*uninterrupted alone time? Thank you, God!*), but to me, an extrovert, there's really nothing worse than feeling lonely and unnoticed by everyone once you step off the stage.

One day I found myself on yet another plane. Getting to my seat near the rear of the plane, I watched as people shoved their massive pieces of luggage into the tiny overhead bins.[1] The introverts around me were putting on their headphones as quickly as possible, attempting to avoid the extroverts (like me) who were thinking about how to strike up a "you're trapped with me now" conversation with the person next to them.

As this was all going on, the flight attendant began to tell us what to do if the plane crash-landed in water.[2] I've heard these instructions plenty of times. But there was something different this time. As I watched, I could tell she was nervous. A middle-aged lady, her voice began to shake as she shared the instructions and safety procedures. She stuttered and had to repeat herself multiple times, fumbling to make it through her words.

It took longer than it should have. The passengers around me began to get impatient and annoyed, murmuring under their breath. Making it through the typical crash-in-water spiel on a flight is hard enough, not to mention trying to sit through a lady struggling to read the script. I remember being a new pastor struggling to read my script (also known as preaching), so I always have a soft spot for those who stumble while speaking in public. It's not as easy as it looks, folks!

As the flight attendant continued, even with her voice shaking, I couldn't help but notice her. Not the words she was saying, but the *person* she was. Typically, I tune out during the safety check (to attempt to talk with the unsuspecting introverts next to me), but this lady's kindness and authenticity were impossible to miss, and I couldn't help but want to listen. It seemed that she truly cared that we heard her instructions. That she wanted us to know what she was sharing. I also hoped that by me listening, she would sense the kindness I felt toward her in the midst of the other passengers' grumblings and wishes that she'd wrap things up quickly. She finished, visibly relieved to be done. She put the phone thing[3] down at the front of the plane and took a breath that I could see from where I was sitting near the back.

Minutes later, the lady quickly passed through the cabin, offering pretzels to the passengers. As she walked by, I gently stopped her and thanked her for sharing the instructions with us.

"You did a wonderful job, Shirley," I said, reading her name tag. Her emotions quickly came to the surface, visible by the tears that showed up in her eyes, and as she stood in the aisle, she started crying, thanking me for my kind words. "I'm newer and this was my first time sharing the preflight instructions on this specific kind of plane. I was so nervous and felt really stupid," she said.

"Well, you did great. It's the first time I've actually listened in months. And as you shared, I could tell you're a wonderful person." She gave me a heartfelt thank-you and continued on to pass out pretzels. For the remainder of the flight I was offered more pretzels and drinks than I could count. Shirley served me in a way no flight attendant had ever served me before. She came back repeatedly to ask if I needed anything else. She checked in on me. Offered to grab whatever I needed. Let me know which gate my next flight was at, even though I wasn't in a hurry.

All because I had noticed her.

I noticed she was nervous.

I noticed she felt foolish.

I noticed she was kind.

I noticed she needed an encouraging word.

I noticed she was a person with a name, not just a talking head at the front of a plane.

I don't know her story, but I began to wonder what made her become a flight attendant at an older age. Maybe it was a job she'd always wanted. But maybe she had recently been through a trial. A divorce? Did she lose a job? Maybe she lost her spouse? Moved to a new city?

I'm thirty-eight, and with each year that passes, change becomes a little scarier. Was she scared? Was this a fresh start for her? Maybe she wondered if a new beginning was even possible? I didn't know. But I noticed her, and in turn, she noticed me.

I wanted her to know this: *I see you're a person. I notice you. I call you by name.*

• • •

It's amazing what happens when we notice someone, but it's even more amazing to watch what happens when someone is noticed by Jesus. Luke, one of Jesus's close friends and the author of one of my favorite books in the Bible, tells us about a woman who suffered from constant bleeding for twelve years.[4] We're never given her name, but she's a woman who Matthew, Mark, and John all mentioned as well—a woman who wasn't noticed by others but was super important to Jesus.

Her illness impacted her not only physically (losing massive amounts of blood is never a good thing, or so I've heard—I'm not a doctor though) but also spiritually. Fellow Jews would have labeled her as "unclean," meaning she wouldn't have been allowed to worship God and go to church (aka the temple). Her bleeding impacted her financially as well—we're told that she spent everything she had on doctors who tried to figure out what was going on with her body. Basically, this lady had tried it all and spent it all, yet her condition only continued to worsen. Few things are more disheartening.

Well, one day Jesus showed up in the town where the woman lived and was immediately greeted by a crowd, a throng of people.[5] A massive amount of people were there, all pressing in, hoping to meet Jesus. But the woman we've been talking about wasn't trying to meet Jesus. She simply wanted to touch him, specifically the very edge of his robe.

Just a little background for us: at this time, touching the edge of someone's clothing was a big deal, and the woman touching Jesus's robe was an even bigger deal. It showed that she believed Jesus was God—that he was God and had the ability to heal her. It might seem strange to us today, but in Jesus's time, the corner of a Jewish person's robe represented his identity, a symbol of who he was and what he stood for. By touching the edge of his robe, this woman was showing that she believed Jesus was the Messiah.

So without anyone noticing, the woman pushed her way through the crowd and she stretched out her hand just enough to touch Jesus. No one else noticed her reaching out her hand, but Jesus did. Immediately he turned around. Someone touched him. The whole crowd was touching him, smothering him. But Jesus noticed the woman's touch and knew it was different.

"Who touched me?" Jesus asked.

"What? Are you joking?" Jesus's friend Peter said. "Who *isn't* touching you is probably the better question. There's a whole sea of people around us. Everyone's touching you, Jesus. The whole crowd has their hands on you." This was way before social distancing! "Stay six feet away from one another and put on some hand sanitizer, please!"

In that moment, the woman knew. She knew she had been noticed, and she worried it was a bad thing. Not wanting Jesus to be upset with her, she quickly explained to him that she thought if she could just touch him, she would be healed.

And it *worked.*

The bleeding stopped—Jesus had healed her. "Your faith has made you well," Jesus told her and then continued walking through the crowd.

To the crowd, it wasn't a big deal. Not one person mentioned the miraculous healing as Jesus continued on his way. But to the woman it was life altering. It changed everything. She was healed and she was noticed.

It's kind of strange to think about, but at some point, that woman died. (At least I haven't seen a two-thousand-plus-year-old lady walking around!) At some point, her health failed her. Jesus didn't heal her forever, making her immune to death or aging. But in that moment of meeting and being healed by Jesus, she was noticed, and that's something I'm sure she never forgot.

• • •

As I've mentioned before, I've worn glasses since I was in kindergarten (remember the four-eyes story?), and I was the first kid in my class to have them. When I take my glasses off, the whole world is a complete blur. I can't see anything or anyone. With my glasses off, in a room full of people, every person's face looks like a garbled mess. Unfortunately, this is how we regularly walk through life. On any given day, the faces of the people we cross paths with are just a blur.

The clients that we work with.

The clerk at the gas station.

The sea of middle schoolers running around when you pick your kids up from school.

All the faces that fly through your Instagram feed.

When people become a blur, their value diminishes—they're no longer human beings. Instead, they're slow drivers keeping us from our agenda. Obstacles that hold us up. Disturbances in the perfect flow of our day. Pests that annoy us. Objects to ridicule and laugh at. Machines for our personal benefit. When people begin to blur, they become obstacles, disturbances, objects, pests, and machines, not people. They become "its."

It's easier not to notice people when they're faceless and nameless. It's easy to be like Peter, who looked at the crowd and said to Jesus, "Who touched you? It's a crowd, it's impossible to tell! Keep walking, Jesus—you can't help them all."

You can't notice everyone, so you end up noticing no one. But when you see a specific person who's hurting, when you find out she's been bleeding for twelve years and just wants to be healed or when you learn he's had a really rough upbringing or when you hear that this is her first time working on a specific plane and she's really nervous—when you see someone as a person like yourself—you can't help but begin to care.

What if we started to notice people? At the jobs we already have. On the blocks where we already live. At the coffee shops we embarrassingly visit multiple times a day (or maybe that's just me).[6]

It might just change the world!

Think about the college or high school student who feels like giving up. What if you noticed him, encouraged him, and told him he'll make it through all the homework and stress and go on to do great things?

Think about the person who never smiles, who might be depressed, who's maybe thinking about killing herself. What if you noticed her—and that was all it took for her to realize that she had a friend, was wanted, was *loved*?

Love notices people. It slows down and sees people, particularly those others overlook. Love takes time out of a busy schedule to smile, to say hi. It holds the door open for people. Love notices when someone's having a bad day and asks, "How are you doing, really?" It looks someone in the eye, communicating *you have my attention and focus*. Love calls people by name. It hurts when someone is hurting and celebrates when someone is celebrating. It sets aside its own agenda and puts another person's agenda first.

Love takes a step back from the crowd and notices who touched the hem of the robe.

Kind of crazy, but as I was writing this specific chapter in a Starbucks in Fargo, North Dakota, I was noticed by two different people. I didn't know a single person in the place, but while I was sitting at the counter, typing away, two separate people came up and asked what I was working on. When I shared, they both individually asked if they could pray for me. They both noticed me. This doesn't seem like much, but I haven't had a random stranger ask to pray for me out of the blue for a couple of years, let alone two people in the span of an hour. I felt loved. I felt cared for. I felt noticed.

Have you ever experienced something like that? Have you ever been noticed when you felt entirely unnoticeable by everyone? Maybe you just moved into college and didn't have a friend to your name, and the girl next to you in class invited you to go to lunch with her. Maybe you felt unappreciated at work when out of the blue your boss called you into his office just to compliment you on the project you completed. Maybe as a stay-at-home mom, you were thinking your family didn't see all the work you did for them, until your son gave you a hug and told you what a great mom you were before bed.

How did you feel in that moment? How did that time, or countless times like it, change you for the better? And how can you, as a result, notice the unnoticeable people in your own life? We've all been there before—the unnoticed, the unwanted, the overlooked. How can you make sure the people in your life, the people you randomly cross paths with on an airplane or in a Starbucks in North Dakota, feel noticed?

• • •

When we landed at the airport and people started to get off the plane, I looked for Shirley. She was standing near the door telling people to have a great day as they were shuffling off. As I approached her, I told her to have a lovely day and thanked her again for her kindness. With tears in her eyes, she said the same to me. It's amazing what noticing someone will do.

Two strangers, among a hundred or so other people, were no longer strangers. Two people felt noticed. Two people, Shirley and I, felt loved.

Love notices people. It calls them by name.

16

Running Man

Love flips the script from anger to grace.

Humans hurt each other. It's what we do. Whether intentionally or not, hurt is bound to happen in any relationship, even with friends and family. Sometimes, though, complete strangers will hurt you out of the blue. You don't know them. You don't know their names or their stories, yet when you cross paths with them or they cross paths with you, they hurt you.

A dirty look. An unkind word. A honk of their car horn accompanied with a hand gesture. Maybe even physical hurt.

• • •

My kids each get paid once a week. If they do all their chores for a week, they each can make a max of four dollars. (Yeah, we're not the best employer in town.)

My daughter normally makes two dollars out of her possible four dollars a week, or three dollars if she was feeling particularly responsible those seven days. But apparently, we're still working on teaching delayed gratification. Because the moment Grayson gets paid, she can't spend her paycheck fast enough. She gets her money, and within minutes she wants to go on a shopping spree. Candy. Gum. ChapStick. It's not super exciting (to a grown-up, at least), but she can't wait.

"Can we go to the store today, Daddy?"

Each week, after a few minutes of trying to convince her to save her money, her cuteness wins me over. She and I walk to Family Dollar, a block from our house. Picture the most pitiful dollar store you've ever seen—uneven floors with tiles that don't match, light bulbs that need to be replaced, trash blowing around the parking lot like tumbleweeds in a western film—that's our Family Dollar. But oddly enough, we love this store. It has everything we could want, a block from our house—including our neighbors. It's a hub of diversity in a town where there isn't much diversity. Every time I go, I see something I haven't seen before. It's a free education!

One specific week, Grayson and I went in with her typical two-dollar paycheck. Walking the aisles, she faces the hardest decision of her week as she figures out what she wants, and this week was no different. Nail polish? Silly Putty? Sour Patch Kids? The usual (gum)?

She finally settled on some Skittles. We paid the cashier, left the store, and started walking home hand in hand. But before we could even leave the parking lot, a man randomly sprinted past us, so fast it seemed like he was trying to beat his time in the fifty-yard dash.

"Where's he going, Daddy?" Grayson asked.

"He must be in a hurry," I said, thinking it seemed a little strange.

We kept walking. Two seconds later, the cashier from Family Dollar also ran past us.

"And where is *he* going, Daddy?!"

"Well, Baby," I said, "I think the first guy must have made a bad decision."

The first dude had clearly just robbed Family Dollar. As the two guys ran off, Grayson seemed a little shaken, but we continued walking toward our house. It was just another day in the neighborhood, and it seemed over. But it wasn't.

All of a sudden, the man who had robbed the store reappeared from behind a house about twenty feet away from us, *sprinting* toward Grayson and me! I quickly pulled Grayson behind me to shield her from Running Man. As he approached, he raised his arm, cocking it back as if he was preparing to punch me right in the face.

There are a bunch of thoughts that run through your mind in this situation:

How did I get here?

Should I go full-on linebacker on this guy?

I haven't been punched by someone since the seventh grade!

Why am I about to be punched?

Why, God?

At the very last second, literally inches from my face, Running Man turned on a dime, darted past, and sprinted away. *What in the world?*

I was untouched, but Grayson wasn't. Though she hadn't been physically hurt, her heart was in turmoil. She ran out into the street full of traffic, screaming! I quickly went and grabbed her as cars stopped right in front of her. She was crying so hard but didn't even make a sound. She was physically shaking, struggling to even walk. I carried her home.

Once I got Grayson home safely, I went to try and help find the man. I couldn't track him down, but I did find the cashier, who immediately asked about Grayson. "Is your daughter okay? I felt terrible about how scared she was!"

Even a random stranger can hurt us. Deeply.

In the days that followed, I struggled to think well of Running Man. It's one thing to hurt me; it's another thing entirely to hurt my daughter. Weeks passed. Grayson is now much more conscious of where we're walking. She no longer wants to go to Family Dollar every week with her paycheck. She's hesitant to walk anywhere outside our house.

. . .

This episode with Grayson and Running Man reminds me of one of the most random people Jesus crossed paths with. But as we know is true with Jesus, nothing is ever really random. On the night before he died on the cross, Jesus met a dude who got his ear cut off.[1] Literally, chopped off with a sword. Ouch![2]

You can't make this stuff up. The man was a soldier, part of the crowd that came to arrest Jesus. Judas betrayed Jesus and gave the mob with him a sign. When the rest of the soldiers moved in to arrest Jesus, Jesus's crew was startled. Specifically, Peter was startled, and without any further thought, he grabbed a sword and slashed off the ear of the guy who tried to arrest Jesus. One startled and hurt person ended up startling and hurting another person.

But then take a look at what Jesus did. Even though he's the one getting arrested, he told his crew, "No more of this!" Instead of doing more harm, Jesus touched the soldier who just got his ear cut off and healed him.[3]

At first glance, it looks like the miracle here is the man's ear growing back, right? But the longer I sit with this strange encounter between this man and Jesus, the more I come to realize that the truly shocking part of the story isn't the healing of the man's ear—it's Jesus's response to what happened. Time and time again, Jesus's response is what makes him so different from me. Otherworldly!

Jesus had just been betrayed by Judas, one of his closest friends. Nothing hurts more than that. Nothing! He's about to be arrested, which will end with him being killed. Peter's response is what we would expect in this situation. As one of Jesus's friends, I probably would have told Peter that he had missed when he cut off only an ear. Aim a little lower next time!

Peter's response is how we would react. At least it's how I would respond. Jesus's response is the miracle. Jesus told his friends to stop getting angry and instead show kindness to the people who were hurting him. Jesus chose kindness over violence, healing over anger. This is grace. This is love.

• • •

My knee-jerk reaction when I'm hurt is to hurt back. Kind of like when you throw your shoe at your neighbor's house after you've had a bad day. (Anyone remember that incident? Only me? Okay, cool.) Particularly when I'm hurt unexpectedly, my reaction is to take a swing at the person. To lash out physically, or at the very least with my words.

Jesus's knee-jerk reaction is to respond quickly as well. But with love.

Jesus responded physically—by *healing* the man, not punching him. Jesus responded to the offense with grace. Notice that Jesus didn't simply tell his friends to stop. Instead he went further, healing the wrong and making it right.

Telling your friends to stop doing something wrong is hard; being kind to the person who wronged you is the supernatural part. How do we know it's supernatural? Because what's natural when someone cuts us off in traffic is to show that person the finger. (I never cease to be amazed by the otherwise sweet people who will quickly throw up the middle finger at another driver.)[4]

When someone says an unkind word, we kick him out of our life, even a longtime friend.

When someone gossips about us, we gossip about her.

We respond tit for tat. An eye for an eye.

If you hurt me, I'll hurt you.

If you hurt my friend, I'll hurt you.

If you don't like me, I won't like you.

If you talk poorly about me, I'll talk poorly about you.

Most would say this is just how the world works.

Jesus would say it's not how *love* works. Love flips the script. It shows people Jesus when all they've seen is anything *but* Jesus. Love practices kindness instead of violence, gentleness instead of lashing out.

When someone assumes the worst of you, assume the best about him.

When someone hurts you, look for ways to help her.

When someone wrongs you, do right by him.

We need to know, without a doubt, that lashing out physically, emotionally, or verbally is never the way of Jesus. Violence is never Jesus's way, and anger is not how he would respond. The word *violence* might not seem like something that applies to you, but I'd argue that we all lash out on a fairly regular basis—these "acts of violence" just happen on a much smaller, seemingly more insignificant scale than scaring a little girl in the street or cutting someone's ear off.

It could be the short-tempered words we say to someone close to us. Throwing a coworker under the bus to get that promotion. With strangers, maybe it's the nasty complaint we leave on the comment card or a thoughtless action toward another.

When you've been hurt, take a deep breath. Most of the time, the reason we're tempted to lash out is because we're overcome with anger and adrenaline. We're tired from going and going 24-7, and our filter is gone. In the heat of the moment, we can easily say or do things we'll later regret. Just take a deep breath.

Don't know the person who hurt you? Remember that the "Running Man" you crossed paths with has a name, even if you don't know it. He's a person too. The guy who scared Grayson might have robbed the store for all kinds of reasons that I don't know about. Maybe he needed food for his kids, or he wanted to have a job and work but wasn't physically able. Those reasons don't make what he did right, but they do change the way I see him.

• • •

That day, I honestly just wanted to punch Running Man in the face. Luckily for Grayson (and my hand!), I didn't get the chance, but that doesn't erase the fact I wanted to. Months have passed since the incident. Grayson is still reluctant to walk with me to Family Dollar. The hurt is still there. As her dad, I don't like that. At all.

But as I sit here, I find myself wondering what would have happened if I had reacted more proactively from a place of love. During the few seconds as he came running toward me with his fist raised, what if I had looked him right in the eyes with a smile of genuine joy on my face? Maybe he would have thought *I* was the crazy one. Or maybe, even just for a second, my smile would have connected with the broken human inside of him. He might have still run off, but maybe it would have been something he wrestled with later. *Why did that man with his little daughter look at me that way? Why was he genuinely smiling at me?* It might seem far-fetched but maybe, just maybe, it could have healed a small part of Running Man that day.

Jesus shows us a different way to treat people who are like Running Man. Honestly, Jesus's way seems far-fetched too. He shows us that love flips the script. Love extends grace when all we want to do is further hurt those who have hurt us. In that moment at Family Dollar, my first reaction wasn't to love the way Jesus would have, yet I did learn something that day, an important lesson about what love looks like when we're facing unexpected hurt and pain. Jesus's story of healing the soldier's ear flipped the script on the way I love in these kinds of situations, and I hope it does for you as well.

So, this is what I'm telling myself. Maybe it applies to you too?

Adam, next time someone tries to hurt you, don't try to cut off his ear.

Heal him.

17

Bill

Love is more than a theory (it's messy).

Throughout my life, I've been great at a lot of things. Actually, not just great—*amazing*. In theory!

Before I was married, I knew exactly how to have an *amazing* marriage. Before I had kids, I constantly felt the temptation to tell actual parents how to parent their kids. My advice would have been *amazing*. Before becoming a pastor and leading a church, I had all the answers. In my head I was the best pastor ever. *Amazing!*

My theory game was strong. I had read books and learned a ton of things. I had seen a bunch of people do all of it. I fully anticipated that I was going to be the best husband, parent, and pastor ever.

Reality woke me up. When I actually tried to be that husband, parent, and pastor, things got messy—really messy—fast. I quickly found out that my wife was a saint for being married to me. When I became a parent, my kids pretty much controlled my life. As for being a pastor, I'm still the most imperfect pastor I know.

The same is true with loving people: love is easy, straightforward, and simple *in theory* but really, really messy in practice. We're all *amazing* at love . . . until we try to do it.[1]

If you end up in a church on any given Sunday, there's a high percent chance you'll hear about loving people.

"Love your neighbor."

"Love the least of these."

"Love God with all your heart, mind, and soul."

"Love." It's an amazing concept (you guessed it) *in theory*. Maybe we take this theory and go on a mission trip or try to love the down-and-out in the nearest big city for a few days. But so often, after we go to church and hear about love, many of us simply return to nice, safe, comfortable neighborhoods filled with people exactly like us, having very few challenges to the "Amazing Love" theories we've been promoting. If there happens to be someone a little rough around the edges walking down our block, thankfully we have garages that we can drive into at the end of the workday, closing the door behind us before we even turn off the car.

Love is great in theory. Great, until it messes up our nice, tidy lives.

I've mentioned before that my neighborhood can be a little interesting from time to time, but the most interesting neighbors we've ever had lived in the rental house directly behind ours.

Two years ago, after our old neighbors moved out of the rental house, our new neighbors moved in: two adult men who seemed like good guys. One of them was Bill, a bigger guy in his mid-thirties who always wore a smile. I introduced myself one day and quickly got to know him.

At first, Bill and his roommate were great neighbors, always friendly and polite. But soon a third and then a fourth person moved into the same house, and the traffic around our block began to increase, along with the number of needles we started to find in the grass. Bill's first roommate had a young son who lived in the house as well, and after a while they moved out. As the roommate was packing up his car, I went over to say goodbye, and he told me that the house was beginning to get a little too crazy for them to stay.

After they moved out, activity around the house went to a whole new level. People were constantly coming and going, day and night, with small packages in hand. Cars were stopping by more frequently than if it were a 7-Eleven gas station, and it was clear something was being sold. (And no, it wasn't Girl Scout cookies.) I would daily pick up armloads of trash around our two houses and still wasn't able to keep up. Empty bottles of alcohol, needles, and trash everywhere.[2] One cop told me, "Your neighbors have everything except a blinking sign that says Drugs." The cops had actually been watching the house for a few weeks and were hoping to catch our neighbors selling whatever it was they were selling.

One night after work, I was walking out of my garage when Bill stopped over to say hello.

"You've maybe noticed that we've had a little traffic lately," he said.

"A little?" I jokingly responded. "I've been tempted to stop over and give you some advice on how to sell drugs! I mean, I did hit the candy cigarettes and Big League Chew pretty hard as a kid."[3]

He blushed, realizing that I fully knew what was going on but wasn't condemning him. "I've been trying to make better decisions, but it's hard," he said. "And . . . you probably know I'm on the sex-offender list. I spent time in prison for doing things with a little kid, but man, I want you to know—I didn't do it."

I didn't tell Bill, but I actually *hadn't* known he was on the sex-offender list. We finished up our conversation and said good night. After getting into my house, I checked the list online.

Yep.

Bill was on it.

• • •

From the start, I had felt led to talk *with* Bill and his friends instead of complaining *about* them.

To care for them.

To drop off chocolate chip cookies.[4]

To try and love them.

This challenged me. Big-time! Love was no longer something nice to talk about on a Sunday morning. Instead it was something I was wrestling with, wondering how to live it out when there were so many days when it was just frustrating. Sure, Bill and his friends were selling drugs, but they were still human. I love what Mother Teresa said: "Help one person at a time and always start with the person nearest to you." Aside from Bec and the kids, that was Bill.

This new information about Bill took things to another level for me, though. I had four kids under the age of thirteen. Finding out Bill was a sex offender (particularly given the crime he was charged with) changed the situation. Later that day, we had a quick family meeting where we reminded the kids about boundaries. We didn't mention Bill or tell them why we were having the family meeting, but we just reminded them to always ask before they went somewhere with anyone and told the younger ones they could only play outside if Mom or Dad was watching or if an older sibling was with them. Nothing is more important to me than my kids and their safety. Nothing!

Yet the first thing I told Bec after Bill said he was on the sex-offender list was, "I don't want this to change anything about the way we look at Bill or treat him. We have to be very smart and careful, especially with the kids, but I want to love him just the same." Once again, Bill is still human, no matter what he was doing or had done in the past. I wanted to love Bill—yes, knowing the truth of what he'd done and being wise around him but also treating him with grace. It was a fine line, but one I chose to walk with Bill.

• • •

When I look at the church and the lives of other Christians (including my own), everything often seems neat and clean. Ideal. Curated. I see good Christian friends who talk about the Bible a lot and wrestle with theology simply for the sake of conversation. Safe lives separated from anything or anyone dirty, shady, or messy. Nice houses. Nice cars. Nice areas of town. The American Dream.

The longer we follow Jesus, the neater, cleaner, and safer our lives seem to become.

Yet in so many ways, the American Dream is very different from the words and actions of Jesus. *So* different. Most of the people Jesus hung out with were messy people living messy lives. Everyone knew how messy they were and did their best to stay away.[5] Jesus hung out with the people others wrote off. He hung out with the people who were living lives completely different from the ones he wanted them to live. And some of the people Jesus crossed paths with didn't magically turn their lives around and live "good Christian lives" either. They stayed messy, yet Jesus still loved them.

Love is messy. Really messy.

It's like eating ribs. I love ribs. They're so good. But there is seriously no clean way to eat ribs. You just have to jump in and get barbecue sauce all over your face. In the same way, we can't wait around and be overly cautious when we love. There's not a clean and pretty way to do it. We just need to hop in and deal with the mess that's there.

A person like Bill is looked down on and shunned by most "respectable" people. He lives in a drug house. Trashing the block is one thing (he and his friends are literally messy), but being a sex offender on top of that is a step further. This label not only puts him low on the totem pole of life; it also puts him at the very bottom of that totem pole in places like prison.

I'll just say it: many would argue that our world would be a lot better off without people like Bill. Any time sex offenders are mentioned in a news story, just check the comments to see how people feel:

"Take them out into the country somewhere, shoot them, and leave them for dead!"

"Drag them behind a car! Sick f—!"

"They should burn in hell!"[6]

It's hard to believe that Jesus loves Bill. Even more so, it's hard to believe that Jesus walks past people like you and me—good Christian people—so that he can befriend, sit with, and hang out with people like Bill.

Read that again. It's hard to wrap our heads around it. Where we condemn, Jesus loves. Where we safeguard our lives, Jesus gets really close. Disgusting, right? Sometimes love looks disgusting.

The truth is, love is complex. It fully protects the innocent while seeking the good of the guilty. To be honest, I called the cops on Bill and his friends fairly regularly. Whenever we saw drug traffic, we called. Whenever someone was yelling at the top of his lungs and it seemed that a war was about to take place in our yard, we called the cops. And truth be told, a large part of the reason I called so many times was because I loved Bill so much. I wanted him to get caught, and if necessary, I wanted him to go back to prison. All because I loved him. He was making bad decisions, and I believed he was better than that.

Even though I was calling the cops, it didn't stop me from going over to say hello to Bill or from sharing my lawn mower when he asked.[7] It didn't get in the way of me dropping off my chocolate chip cookies. With Bill, love was no longer a theory. It got messy. Yet interacting with Bill strangely made me feel closer to Jesus.

• • •

If you're a Christian and your life looks perfectly neat and clean, you might want to make sure you're actually following Jesus. If there's no one in your life who's messy or really hard to love, I'd encourage you to start putting yourself in places where you can meet people like Bill. The hard, messy places.

Maybe you end up selling your house in the burbs to move somewhere "shady."

Maybe it's coming alongside another adult to help him get his life back on track.

Maybe it's befriending that addict.

Maybe it's reaching out to someone who you know is making bad choices and grabbing coffee together.

Maybe it's letting someone who's getting back on her feet stay in your extra guest bedroom.[8]

Maybe it's being present with the person who had an affair.

I pray that your life and the friends you hang out with after leaving church on Sundays would be messy, not clean. The longer we follow Jesus, the messier—not cleaner—our lives should become. That's when the sermon and your own walk with Jesus will be put to the test.[9]

Keep boundaries but don't condemn. This might seem to contradict the entire chapter, but we do need boundaries in our lives. Boundaries are good and they're necessary, especially if we're new to following Jesus or if there's an area we have a particularly hard time with.

Struggle with drinking? Stay away from the bar and friends who drink regularly. Are you married but attracted to someone who's not your spouse? It's not your responsibility to help that person. Instead, connect him or her with a friend. Healthy boundaries are so important.

We greatly undervalue the power of prayer for the people in our lives. Sometimes we're just not qualified to deal with the issues that people are dealing with. So, we instead love them and pray urgently for them—asking God to bring freedom in their lives, asking him to help them make changes and motivate them to get help. Even with the people we do feel "qualified" to help, prayer should be our first resort, not our last. Who are the people you're regularly praying for?

• • •

Six or seven months ago, the cops were stopping by our neighborhood so often that Bill and his friends finally moved out. The house was left empty. I'd be lying if I didn't say this was at least a little bit of a relief for us.

I no longer had to worry about the kids finding needles in the grass or pick up an entire bag full of trash on my lawn every other day. I no longer had to think about having a sex offender in my backyard. Strangely enough, though, I miss Bill.

I miss his smile. I miss the conversations we had as I got out of my car at the end of the workday while he sat on his front porch. I guess you could say I loved him. We miss the people we love and care for. I don't miss the mess, though. At all. The drug activity, trash, and craziness.

But I do miss the person who was a mess.

I don't miss the mess, but I miss the messy man.

• • •

A few weeks passed, and I randomly reached out to the owner of the rental house to see what her plans were for it.

"We don't want to do rentals anymore, so we're thinking about selling," the owner told me.

"Really? What would you need moneywise for it?" I asked.

"Let's get an appraisal and start there. You might also want to see the inside of the place first. It's a mess."

She wasn't kidding. The ceiling in the kitchen was falling in. The carpets were destroyed. The entire house smelled like urine, even though Bill and his roommates didn't have pets. A couple windows were broken. It was truly a disgusting mess!

Why would we ever be interested in buying a house that was literally falling apart? We planned on restoring it and then listing it as an Airbnb. But the main reason we'd consider buying it? To have a place available in case a friend is going through a messy season of life.

Maybe for a friend walking through an unexpected trial who needs some extra help. A family that doesn't have anywhere to go. A person trying to get back on track. A friend who needs a place to stay for a few weeks.

How cool would it be for this rental house to go from being a drug house to a place of refuge? To change from a place of brokenness to a place of healing? Hopelessness to hope. Darkness to light.

A house that was a mess could maybe feel like a home for someone walking through a mess.

More than a house getting a makeover, Jesus longs for the same thing to happen inside of people like Bill, inside of people like you, and inside of people like me.

Years ago, we bought a piece of land and built the cutest little lake cabin ever. It's a spot filled with memories, our dream setup. But the only way we could afford to flip the old drug house in our backyard was by selling the cabin. No matter how hard we tried not to think about it, God kept nudging us. When I posted the listing for the cabin on Facebook, Bec starting crying. That cabin meant so much to us. Even though she completely agreed to sell it, it was still hard to let that dream go.

When the owners of the drug house got the appraisal done, it was a fair value but one we couldn't afford. I explained it was out of our price range and encouraged them to list it. I knew it would sell quickly. They responded, "We want to hear your offer first."

"What? Why? You can sell it for that price!"

"We want to hear your offer first."

"You promise you won't be upset with a low offer?"

"We promise. We want to hear it."

I gave them our offer, thousands less than the appraisal, and needless to say, we're now the proud owners of a drug house—a former drug house!

Our cabin quickly sold, and the drug house was officially ours. As I type this, my hands are covered in paint. This week the wood floors are getting restored.[10]

Just to be clear, there's no need to think we're anything special. Anyone who knows us can tell you the same thing. We bought the house because we felt it was something God wanted us to do.

We decided we no longer wanted love to be a theory. My only hope is that if someone took a close look at my *life*—not just my beliefs, theology, and church attendance—they'd see Jesus all over the place.[11]

I still have no idea whether this is a terrible idea or not. But I do know that it sounds messy, really messy, and I think that's what Jesus wants love to look like.

18

Russ and F-Man

Love makes the least important the most important.

A little while ago, I somehow ended up going to an MMA fight. I'm not into recreational fighting, and honestly, I don't really know how to feel about MMA. Is it okay for two dudes to climb into an octagon and basically try and kill each other while the crowd roars? I mean, some people are pretty vocal that it should be illegal. Personally, I'm more of a lover than a fighter (other than when petty thieves are about to punch me in front of a dollar store).

But earlier that week, I had randomly met one of the fighters,[1] and then another person offered me two free tickets to go see the Friday night fight.[2] I texted a friend, asking if he wanted to go with me. He said sure.[3]

So, Friday night came, and there I was, pulling into the arena parking lot, wondering what I had gotten myself into. As soon as we parked, I turned to my friend and asked, "Should we even be here?"

"We probably won't even see anyone we know," he said, trying to reassure me.

As soon as we stepped through the doors of the arena, things got crazy! Ninety-five percent of the crowd was guys. Beer flowed like water. The testosterone level was off the charts. Oh, and two dudes were getting ready to kill each other on the mat. No big deal, right?

We tried to find our seats in the chaos. *Let's just try to fly under the radar,* I thought. *Play it cool, Adam. Everything will be fine.*

But while we made our way to our seats, it seemed like every person in the arena was saying hi to me.

"Adam!"

"Pastor!"

"Hey, man! Hey! I go to Embrace!"

What in the world?! It seemed like every other dude there was either saying hi to me or extending his hand to shake mine. All I could think was, *Is our entire church at this fight? Maybe this is our new Friday night service?*

The best moment came when my friend and I finally got to our seats in the third row (at this point, we were pretty much in the ring). The guy sitting right next to me caught my eye. He was staring at me, with a huge smile. *Did he know me somehow? Did he sense I wasn't a fighter and want to beat me up?* I kind of gave him a quick nod as a way of saying hello, and in response he said, "Hey, man! You're my f—ing pastor!"

(Just to be clear, he didn't say I was his "favorite" pastor.)

I responded, "Really? You go to Embrace?"

"Yeah," he replied. "I actually hate going to church, but my wife dragged me there a few months back. Now I absolutely love going! Each week, I feel like the message is speaking right to me."

The lights went down, and the fight got ready to start. But it was the man's words that stuck in my head. *"You're my f—ing pastor."* I laughed. *Yes, man, I am. And I think that's a good thing.*

As I watched the fight, I thanked God that my new friend felt he could be real around me. He wasn't fake. He didn't turn into some kind of angel like a lot of people do when they find out I'm a pastor. Instead, he was just himself—a dude at an MMA fight who was excited (*really* excited apparently!) to see his pastor there next to him.

Honestly, I don't think I'd ever been so proud to be someone's (f—ing) pastor. I was so thankful he had introduced himself, so thankful he had said hello.

That night, that fight was exactly where I needed to be.

• • •

One of Jesus's close friends, a dude named Matthew, tells us about a time when Jesus was leaving the town of Jericho to go to Jerusalem for an important celebration.[4]

As Jesus was leaving town, a large group of people were following behind him. They were excited for the extravagant parade that would take place, with Jesus as the central focus. But behind the crowd of people were two men sitting alongside the road. We don't know the names of these two men—all we're told is they were blind.[5]

Sitting near the edge of the road, these men were most likely beggars. The lowest of the low in society. But when they heard that Jesus was coming their way that day, they began to cry out, "Lord, have mercy on us!" They probably had heard that Jesus had the ability to heal people miraculously, and they hoped to be healed of blindness too.

When the two men cried out, the crowd reacted harshly toward them, yelling for them to be quiet. Jesus clearly had more important things to do than pay attention to two blind beggars. He was on his way to Jerusalem for some important business there. If he had to stop, it wouldn't be for two blind guys on the side of the road, obviously!

My translation of what the crowd yelled: "Shut up, you two blind, worthless men!"

But the men didn't care what the crowd thought. Being told to be quiet only made them shout louder. I love it. These guys are feisty! Read between the lines—you can almost hear their thoughts: *You're telling us to shut up? Well, unfortunately for you, do we look like we give a rip what you think? Nope, not at all!*

Here, once again, Jesus does the unexpected. Rather than listening to the crowd and continuing on his way, rather than talking with the most important folks there, Jesus instead heard the two men and he stopped, not letting the cry of the needy—the cry even of two blind beggars—go unheard. Jesus stopped, and going one step further, he asked, "What do you want me to do for you? You name it, and I'll do it."

They do.

And he does.

• • •

A couple of years ago, a guy I knew from high school named Russ started coming to Embrace. In junior high we were friends through sports, but after high school I heard his life got pretty wild. As a result, this guy turned into one of the craziest dudes ever. Like an intense, I-will-mess-you-up, mean-looking dude.

I'll never forget the first Sunday Russ came to Embrace. His wife had brought him there, and I was completely shocked to see him. But what I remember most is that when I went to say hello before the service, Russ didn't even acknowledge I was there. It was pretty clear he didn't want to be in church.

But he and his wife started coming regularly, and more and more I could see God at work in his life. Even though he wouldn't say it, I could see something changing in him.

As we walked into the MMA fight that night, I saw Russ and told the friend I was with that I wanted to make sure I said hello before the end of the night. His dad had died a month or so earlier, and I had been praying for him.

Halfway through the night, someone tapped me on the shoulder. I turned around to find Russ standing there! I couldn't believe he had come up to me. I asked how he was doing and shared that I was so sorry to hear about his dad. He said, "Honestly, even though I'm in the middle of this crappy situation of losing my dad, I can see God at work. It's almost like God was preparing my dad and he was preparing me for this to happen. I feel God has really been at work in my life lately." He finished by thanking me for praying for him and his family. I was speechless.

As he walked away, the "you're my f—ing pastor" guy (remember him?) sitting next to me quickly asked, "How do you know that guy?" I told him it was also through Embrace. "Really?" he asked. "That's one of the craziest guys ever. Like, insane! But about a year or so ago, he started changing. I've always wondered what happened to make him change like that."

I didn't say it then, but I knew the answer. Among a few things, it was God. God was at work in Russ's life and was changing him from the inside out.

• • •

When Jesus had heard the two men shouting, he stopped and asked, "What do you want me to do for you?"

"We want to see!" they replied.[6]

The men said exactly what they're feeling.

They *didn't* say, "Well, Jesus, we really just want to hear more information about you. Can you tell us your favorite passages of Scripture?" They didn't butter Jesus up. They didn't start talking religiously and bow down and worship him.

Nope. None of that.

They simply said, "We're blind, and we just want to see."

Their directness is refreshing, and it reminds me of the guys at the MMA fight.

"You're my f—ing pastor."

"I actually hate going to church, but my wife dragged me there a few months back. Now I absolutely love going!"

"Even though I'm in the middle of this crappy situation of losing my dad, I can see God at work."

The two blind men just said what they felt. And Jesus responded. He felt compassion for them and touched their eyes. Instantly, they could see. Matthew tells us of other times where Jesus felt compassion for people, but in every case except this one, Jesus felt compassion for *crowds* of people. This time, that compassion was specific to these two men. That's pretty cool.

There's more. The part that's often overlooked in this story of Jesus and the blind beggars is what happened after he healed them. Unlike *all* the other times when Jesus healed someone and then continued on his way, only for the healed person to stay behind, we're told that the two men got up and *followed* Jesus! They wanted to be part of what Jesus was doing. They got up, left their lives behind, and followed him. This is the only occurrence we're told about where someone was healed by Jesus and then immediately followed him.

· · ·

At the MMA fight, I understood a glimpse of how Jesus must have felt. Compassion for two specific guys, as rough around the edges as they were. Maybe the two in the crowd I was the *least* likely to feel compassion toward, all things being equal.

The two blind men that Jesus encountered were seen as unimportant and useless by those around them. They just didn't fit the mold. Instead they were loud—asking Jesus to heal them in a way many would probably be afraid to do. Russ and F—Man are a lot like the two blind men. Rough and unpolished, they make most "church" people feel pretty uncomfortable. So the church doesn't make space for them. We ignore them until they go away or at least until they clean up their lives, or we end up telling them they can't ask certain questions or say certain things. We think these types of people don't belong in a church. Oh, except for the fact that *God* thinks they're important—the most important, not the least.[7]

Love makes the least important the most important.

So how do we love people like Russ and F—Man? People like the blind men in Matthew? How do we elevate these "least important" people in our lives to the VIP status they already have with God?

First, we have to acknowledge them. That night at the fight, I could have chosen to intentionally ignore F—Man when he told me I was his you-know-what pastor. Worse yet, I could have called him out for using that kind of word to describe me. *You can't swear! If you go to church, you would know that you should really stop swearing!*[8] Case closed. Conversation done.

Instead, as Jesus did with the two men on the road, I acknowledged F—Man. I said hi to him. I asked him questions; I listened to his story and genuinely got to know him in the process. Love that makes the least important the most important starts by acknowledging people.

Second, stop caring what everyone else thinks. Easier said than done, right? Tell me about it. I struggle with this too. Remember how I almost didn't go to the fight? *Wait, that's the pastor at Embrace? And he's talking to those guys? I know what type of guys they are, and he's friends with them?!* When loving people with this least-important-to-most-important kind of love, we have to—and I mean, really have to—stop caring what x, y, and z person and his dog think of us. It doesn't matter, and just as in the case of Jesus with the blind men, it only slows us down. Imagine if Jesus had cared what the crowd thought about him stopping to heal two blind beggars. Matthew wouldn't have had a story to tell! Stop caring what other people think and love the least important in your life.

Lastly, remember that you, too, are one of these least important people. Yep, you!

But, Adam, I have a six-figure income!

I've accomplished this whole laundry list of things, and I'm not even that old yet!

You don't realize it, but I've actually done a ton of good things in my life.

Adam, how could I possibly be one of the least important people? Don't you know who my parents are?!

Trust me, you're not that big of a deal. Honestly, none of us are, and it's when we realize this that we're better equipped to love everyone equally, without looking down on them and thinking we're better than them.

Fully coming to terms with being one of "the least of these" is faith altering. It gives us an attitude of humility in everything we do, including how we choose to love other people. While we might not be that big of a deal, everyone we come in contact with can be (and is!). The only logical way we can choose to respond to them, then, is in love—a love that treats everyone like the VIPs they are in God's eyes.

Russ and F—Man were only looking for one thing: to be loved—and to be loved well. There are so many least important people in our everyday lives just waiting to be loved, like the two blind men who wanted healing and believed Jesus could love them that way.

Today, let's choose a love that makes the least important the most important.

19

A.C. Kidd

Love pulls up a chair.

A few years back, after one of the morning services at church, a college kid—let's call him A. C. Kidd[1]—approached me and asked, "What's your stance on homosexuality?"

Regardless of where a person stands on the subject, I'd much rather have an actual conversation than throw my answer at you. But when A. C. asked his question, he wasn't interested in a conversation. He wanted my verdict. Fast. So, I gave him my twenty-second elevator-speech answer. He responded, "Thanks," turned, and walked away. I remember thinking to myself, *I have no clue where he's at, but regardless, there's a strong chance he's not crazy about my answer!*

I went home, not thinking anything more of A. C., took my one-hour power nap as I do every Sunday, and then went back to the church for the evening service. After the service, I headed up to my office to gather all my things before going home and calling it a night.

As I was packing up, I looked out my office door and saw a staff person trying to slow a man down as he walked as quickly as he could toward me. The guy got past the staff person, came into my office, and whipped around me so fast I didn't even realize who it was until he turned around.

It was A. C. Kidd! "I have another question!" he quickly blurted out.[2]

Startled and shocked (and honestly, a bit scared) by how quickly he had made it into my office and by the fact that he was now farther into the room than I was, all I could say was "Well, let's hear it!"

"How can you live with yourself pastoring a church full of people who are damned to hell?" he demanded. "This morning there were two gay guys holding hands in your church, and I'm just wondering how you could possibly welcome them here!"

Now, I'm not a very confrontational person. Let's rephrase that: the mere *thought* of conflict makes me want to curl up in the fetal position. If you see a conflict, I'll be running in the opposite direction. But for some reason, in that moment, I just felt I was supposed to speak up. Not about my viewpoint on a certain topic but instead about the pride I could sense in A. C. Kidd's voice. I gently responded, "That's a great question, and it sounds exactly like something that was said in the Bible."

He looked puzzled, so I continued, "Yep, this sounds exactly like Luke chapter 15 verse 2.[3] Jesus was sitting with tax collectors and sinners, while the Pharisees were grumbling and mumbling about Jesus welcoming those guys and eating with them. You know that story, don't you?"

"Yep," he quietly replied.

I could tell A. C. knew the Bible well, so I continued on by asking, "Do you know about the tax collectors?"

"Yes, they overtaxed their own people."

"That's true, but picture this," I said. "I don't know your dad, but I'm sure he's a great man. Now imagine me stealing money from your dad. Every single day, your dad works hard, and I just work harder and harder to steal his money. How would you feel about me?"

"I wouldn't like you," he said.

"You're getting close, but we're still not there. Now picture your mom *and* your dad, and I'm stealing every penny I possibly can from both of them. Taking every cent I can get my hands on. I arrogantly laugh and thank God that they both work hard and make money so that I can spend it all on myself, leaving them with little. Now how would you feel about me?"

With an intense look I've never seen before in a person's eyes, he said, "I would *hate* you!"

I smiled. "Now you're starting to understand the story. Now picture me coming home and God throwing the craziest party ever to celebrate my return. God is so thankful that his beloved son has come home. He loves me dearly and is rejoicing at my arrival! This is the story in Luke 15. And the truth is—it isn't a pretty story, is it? It's not even a nice story. It's appalling. It's wrong. It's disgraceful!

"That is, until we realize . . . it applies to us. Back to your question about welcoming certain people, you want to know who I can't believe we let in church today? I'm almost embarrassed that we let him in. I really can't believe it! It's sickening to even think about."

"Who?"

"You! I can't believe we let *you* in here. I don't know you, but I'm sure there are some things in your private life that disqualify you from being here, things from your past that would shock me if I heard them. I can't believe we let you in here. Unreal! But now that I think about it, there's one other person who's even *worse* than you. I'm actually going to talk with my staff to make sure this person never gets in here again for church. Do you know who that is?"

A. C. quietly asked, "Who?"

"Me! I've made so many mistakes. I can't *believe* some of the things I've said and done. I'd be so embarrassed to share it all. Honestly, I should never be let into this church ever again. But that's a lot to take in, isn't it?"

"That's a lot to take in."

A. C. quietly walked out the door, leaving my office. I stood there, shocked that I had said all that. But I meant every word.

• • •

The truth is, there are a lot of things that have and will be debated for centuries. Particularly in the church.

Free will versus predestination.

Baptizing versus dedicating your kid.

Democrat versus Republican.

Adam and Eve—real versus a metaphor.

Traditional marriage versus gay marriage.

Bengals versus Steelers.[4] (Pray for Steelers fans. They're clearly living in sin!)

I'm grateful to know a lot of wonderful, God-fearing people on both sides of these issues. We can disagree on a lot of things, but if we've read our Bibles for longer than five seconds, we know we don't get to decide whom we welcome and whom we love. God does. And his answer? *Everyone.*

The world responds to hate with more hate. Just as A. C. Kidd wanted to damn certain people to hell.

You voted for this person and I voted for that person? I hate you!

You think this and I think that? I hate you!

You're passionate about this and I'm passionate about that? I hate you!

You disagree with me on x, y, or z? I hate you!

Jesus turns things upside down. He makes it clear: I disagree with you. I don't agree with your actions. I think very differently than you.

Your ways are not my ways—they're different. But get this: I still want to sit with you. I still welcome you. I still love you.

Welcoming people is different from agreeing with people. Loving people doesn't mean changing what we believe. It doesn't mean watering down God or the Bible. It doesn't mean agreeing with others when we know we don't.

But what if we put as much effort into finding common ground as we do into picking apart one another's arguments? What if instead of automatically focusing on what makes us different, we choose to celebrate what makes us the same? To listen? To respect instead of belittling someone else's point of view? What if we loved one another as broken, messed-up people and not just because we fall on the same side of the political spectrum?

What if we pulled up a chair next to someone instead of damning him to hell?

Do people know what you're for or do they just know what you're against? My opinion is that we already have enough "against" people—people who only talk about what they don't agree with. I want to be one of the "for" people—people constantly focused on the positive things we're for, not what we're against.

Do you disagree with someone? Instead of distancing yourself or condemning her to hell in your head, befriend her. Sit down and listen to her. It's harder to hate someone after you've grabbed coffee with her. And it's more difficult to judge when you've heard her story and not just the pretty parts.

Here's something to consider: Do the people who disagree with you still enjoy being with you? Better yet, do you have many friends, not just acquaintances, who disagree with your thoughts and beliefs? Don't have any? That's not a good thing. I love you enough to tell you, in this area of your life you don't look like Jesus—at all! We should be surrounding ourselves with people who are different from us.

Too often we write off people we don't agree with as being evil, but is that really our job? Is our job to poke holes in every opinion that doesn't totally line up with ours? Often we'd rather tear people down than simply try to understand.

. . .

Something that sticks out to me about Jesus is that when he's sitting with tax collectors and sinners (or anyone he disagrees with, for that matter—with the exception of religious people), he doesn't immediately start talking about their obvious shortcomings and differences. He doesn't sit down and talk about how he disagrees with what the tax collectors do for a living. He doesn't discuss their sin or explain his viewpoint in a condescending, trying-to-win-an-argument sort of way. Nope, Jesus loves them.

Jesus pulls up a chair.

He pulls up a chair and sits with them. He asks them questions. He teaches them about God—about his grace, truth, love, and joy. He shows them the gaps that exist between who he is and who they are. He eats food with them. (Crazy idea: maybe we should grab Chipotle with the people we disagree with.)[5]

Foreign, right? As I'm writing these words, it bothers me a bit. *But what about their sin? Jesus, they're stealing people's money! And now you're sharing this story about God's incomprehensible love and grace with them? It doesn't make sense! You need to confront them. You need to challenge them. Right now!*

But Jesus simply sits down and loves them. He never says that what they're doing is okay. He doesn't say he's cool with their lives and tell them "just do what you feel." He doesn't sign off on their crap, their sin. But he loves them. And he loves them so well.[6] Even though it's clear that Jesus is otherworldly, that he's holy and they are not. Even though he is so different, they are irresistibly drawn to him and want to be as close to him as they can possibly get.

I've found that love has a way of changing everything about a person. Arguments? Nope, I've never seen a person change because of an argument. Hate? Nope, I've never seen hate change a person's life for the better. But love? I've seen love change the hardest people, including myself. I've seen love change the way people think and vote. I've seen it change convictions and beliefs. I've seen love change the way people live.

Just so we don't miss it: Jesus tells the story of the party-throwing father and his lost son, the story I shared with A. C.—not for the sinners and tax collectors to hear (although I'm sure it would have made them feel so loved)—but for the grumbling religious people to hear. For A. C. Kidd and you and me to hear. It's a story that steps on toes. Jesus challenges the religious people. Why? Because he loves them too. He challenges them because he loves them.

As the party for the younger brother takes place, the father goes out to the older brother and invites him in too. It's more than an invitation, though. The dad *begs* his older son to come inside. He yearns for him to fully experience his love, grace, and freedom too. He so badly wants the older brother to join the party!

That day when I spoke those words to A. C. Kidd, my deepest hope was that God would move in him. Hearts and lives filled with anger aren't what God has for us. A. C. is as welcome as anyone is. God loves him so much. Even when you and I are like A. C. Kidd, God loves us too. Even in our pride and arrogance, he begs us to come home.

Love doesn't damn people to hell. Love pulls up a chair.

20

Ted, Ambrase Lekol, Jillian, and Jerry

Love makes every day an adventure.

Confession: I'm a control freak.

Truth be told, I spend most of my days trying to control things.

How clean my house is (which is not easy with four kids).

How others view me (which becomes harder the more people you know).

How nice my beard looks (beard oil, anyone?).

Basically, I try and control everything. Every single day.

You think I'm bad? I hate to be the one to tell you this, but you're kind of a control freak too. We humans, we try to control it all. We try to control our image, online and offline. We try to control how our body ages with creams, surgeries, and weird diets. We even try to control other people, and it's pretty easy to see how well that works out for us.

But more than my image or my age, what I really want to control is my *time.*

I want to follow Jesus with everything I have, sure. And I'm making some progress. I gave up my dream of running a company to become the pastor of a church I didn't want to start. I started tithing while getting my master's degree (in other words, I gave money away to a church when I was pretty much broke). I've forgiven people who have hurt me in ways that I never could have imagined.

All this to say, I've tried to give God everything. But maybe the hardest thing for me to turn over to Jesus has been my *time*—handing over my daily agenda for his.

I have meetings to be at. Deadlines to hit. Sermons to write. Bills that have to be paid. A lawn that needs to be mowed. And kids who require three meals a day to survive. (Okay, truth be told, my wife is the only reason my kids eat and are still alive.)

The older I get, the more I've realized how little control I actually have. At some point, I stopped trying to do what I want to do. Instead, each morning I simply ask God what his plan is. *God, what do you want me to do today? Whom do you want me to meet with? How can I join you in what you want to do today? Where do you want me to go?*

This daily practice of handing control over to God is why I'm here right now, hanging out at a table on the sidewalk. As I type this, I'm sitting at one of the busiest intersections in Sioux Falls: Tenth Street and Phillips Avenue. I have a wooden suitcase that folds out to become a desk (you can find anything on the internet), a plant, a bobblehead of a baseball player, and a framed picture of my wife. With two chairs on each side of the desk, it's like a mini portable office.

Oh, and I have a sign that sits on the desk that says, "Need to talk? Pull up a chair."[1]

Yep, people walking by are giving me weird looks, but I'm strangely okay with it![2] Maybe this was something God asked me to do with my time, or maybe my lemon LaCroix was spiked, but either way, I find myself sitting here, my time open and available if someone needs to talk.[3]

What I'm beginning to realize is that life turns into an adventure when we simply stop and ask God what his plan is instead of following our own agenda for the day. I'm not talking about an adventure like the exotic trips they take on *The Bachelor*. Instead, it's an adventure that might appear normal but that I'd argue is supernatural.

Our lives are often a lot like the movie *Groundhog Day*. We do the same things over and over and over. We spend days, months, years, and decades of our lives knowing for the most part exactly what those days, months, years, and decades will bring.

Alarm clock. Go to the bathroom after holding it for hours. Let the dogs out.[4] Shower. Eat breakfast. Drive to work. Clock in. Work. Eat lunch. Clock out. Go home. Eat dinner. Watch TV. Go to bed. Repeat.

Now, there's nothing wrong with doing the same thing every day. In this ever-changing world, there's actually something appealing about faithfully working the same job for thirty years, living in the same house for generations, and grabbing coffee with the same group of friends at the same coffee shop every morning. Really, there's nothing wrong with that. We need more of that!

But what's normal, including our routines, becomes supernatural when we simply allow Jesus to take control of how we spend our time. It's truly amazing what God will do if we let him.

Most people wish their lives had a little more adventure. Most people hope for something more than the nine-to-five. Most people want to be used by God. They're just not sure where to start.

Ted.

As I was pulling out of my garage to go to work a few weeks back, I crossed paths with a couple of young neighbor kids who were shooting baskets into the hoop on their driveway.

I rolled down my window as I was driving past. "Nice hoop!" I said, as a way of saying hi to the boys.

The older-looking kid (who I'd later find out was Ted's friend) quickly responded, "Why don't you get us a new hoop?"

I looked up to see that the backboard on the hoop was broken and that the whole thing was struggling to stay upright. It was honestly pretty sad looking.

At first, I was taken aback by the kid's sassy answer. *The punk actually wants me to get him a new hoop? Get your own hoop, kid.*

But a few minutes later I heard God say, *Actually, why don't you get them a new hoop, Adam?*

Oh. *Okay, God.*

A few hours later, I mentioned the new hoop to a friend.[5] After our conversation, I posted on Facebook about the neighbor boys and their broken-down hoop, asking if people wanted to help.

Immediately people started responding. Within an hour, I had a hoop in perfect condition that a single mom wanted to give away, two basketballs, some other gear from a local head basketball coach, and a pickup truck from a guy who was willing to go get the hoop and drop it off for the boys.

Crazy.

The next day, I stopped by the house where the neighbor boy named Ted lived and knocked on the door. His mom answered, and I asked if she would be willing to step outside and talk. I told her that I'd seen that their basketball hoop was in rough shape and that someone was going to drop off a new hoop and basketball gear.

The mom quickly changed from looking defensive, worried her son had done something wrong, to being overjoyed.

"You don't need to do this," she said.

"Actually, I do need to," I said, explaining that the idea for the new hoop didn't come from me.

I went on to say that the only stipulation with the hoop was that I wanted it to be a gift from her to her boy and his friend. She would be the hero, not us. She was speechless.

The next day came and the basketball coach dropped off two basketballs, two awesome gym bags, and two Sioux Falls Roosevelt High School Rough Riders basketball shirts. Later, the hoop arrived in the back of a pickup truck of a guy whose son was battling cancer.

"Thank you for letting me help deliver this hoop," he said. "It feels really good to do something nice for someone else when so many nice things have been done for us."

Weeks have passed, and daily the boys are outside shooting hoops. I honestly thought they'd maybe enjoy it for a few days and then move on to the next thing. Even if that was the case, it still would have been worth it—because when we do something that God tells us to do, there shouldn't be any strings attached, no expectations of even receiving a thank-you. Instead the boys are out there shooting hoops for hours. It's fantastic.

Love makes every day an adventure.

When I planned my day the morning I drove past the boys with the sad-looking hoop, I had no idea I'd spend that day looking for a new basketball hoop. God's plan for the day and my time was so much better than my own.

Ambrase Lekol.

A few years back, a group of people from Embrace took a missions trip to Haiti. I wasn't planning on going along and was actually looking for reasons to skip the trip. If I was going to go somewhere for eight days, hopefully it'd be a relaxing paradise. I had heard that Haiti was beautiful but anything but a relaxing paradise. Nonetheless, I felt obligated to go if our church was going to do future trips, so I signed up.

I went on the trip, having no idea what would come of it. Our job as a team was to help take pictures of the students at the mission so they could be sponsored. One of the groups of kids we met with didn't have a school building, so they gathered daily under a tree for class. I immediately began feeling the nudge to ask the director questions.

"When are you hoping to build a school?" I asked.

"Someday in the future would be nice, but we don't have the money," she said.

"Well, how much would it cost? Do you know where you'd build it?"

"We actually have a piece of land," she said.

The moment I saw the land was the same moment I knew Embrace would be helping them construct a school building. Today, a couple hundred kids fill that building each week. A new well provides clean water. Teachers are teaching. Cooks are cooking food. Kids are learning and becoming students. Adults are practicing trades to earn an income.

The school was built concrete block by concrete block, thanks to a team of Haitian contractors, and now this one small school has impacted an entire village called Jabouin—and really, an entire region of Haiti. The village was so thankful for the building that they decided to name the school Ambrase Lekol (The Embrace School).

Fast-forward to a couple of months ago, when another staff person and I met with the Jabouin school administrators to get an update on the school. The school and students themselves were doing well, but the space was maxed out. Some kids, including kids as young as first grade, were walking three hours to school (one way!) simply because this was the closest school to where they lived.[6]

"We keep praying that God will provide a way to build a new school," one of the administrators said to me.

Now, there are times when you need to pray and discern the will of God. This wasn't one of those times. Sometimes God speaks loud and clear through a Haitian school administrator who wants to provide kids with an education.

"Okay," I said. "Let's hear about this new school." (I couldn't get those words out fast enough.)

"There's a village called Madame Pierre that has no school," he said. "Some of the kids walk from that village all the way to the Jabouin school. If we built a school in Madame Pierre it would cut their walk from three hours down to fifteen minutes. The village wants a school so badly, they told us they'd donate the land if someone could pay for the school."

"How much does it cost to start the school?"

"We can start with four classrooms. For kids pre-K to first grade it would be $25,000."

"I'll see what we can do," I said.

I started kicking around ideas about the new school and made plans to reach out to a few friends, people I thought might be interested in giving to the project.

That was my plan, until one Sunday morning when I randomly decided to mention the school project at church. Within three days, we had raised more than $30,000 for the school, and I was having to turn people away. We emailed the school administrators and told them the money was on its way and to start building the school![7]

I hadn't planned on spending my time raising money for a school in Haiti, but God had. I didn't even want to go on that initial trip, but I'm so glad God got me on the plane. Once again, when I stopped holding my time so tightly, an adventure began.

Jillian.

A few weeks ago, I got this random idea to build a short wall-fence thing in one of the back alleys near my house and paint some angel wings on it. Weird, right? I've seen wings on the sides of buildings in other cities that are great for photo ops, and I decided I'd try doing the same thing. Art seems to have a way of encouraging and uplifting people, plus I'd been looking for ways to convince locals to come visit the area where I live, so this seemed like a good idea.

I had a firefighter I know build the wall,[8] I painted it white, and then I posted on Facebook in search of an artist to paint the actual wings. Fifteen minutes later, I had a Sioux Falls artist named Jillian coming over to paint. I love the World Wide Web!

Later that week, Jillian was in the back alley. She drew out the wings on a notebook, and once it was dark enough, she set up a projector, pointed it at the wall, and traced out the wings in black paint.

I stayed outside and talked with Jillian as she painted—partly because I didn't feel comfortable with her being alone in the back alley after dark and partly because I'm an extrovert and wanted to hear her story.

She finished the wings, and they looked even better than I had hoped. Within the first few days of being done, every news station in town had done a story on the wings. But better than the fun publicity, I got to meet neighbors I didn't know I had when they stopped by to see the wings.[9]

A young girl named Kali took her picture with the wings to celebrate her completed leukemia treatment.

Groups of friends took selfies together and posted parts of their stories.

An older man named Carney had us use his flip phone to take a photo of him.

People took pictures of their family dogs.

A bride stopped by on her wedding day.

A senior stopped by in her graduation gown.

One lady even took a photo of her bike! She must have really loved that bike.

It was incredible. But my favorite message came from Jillian herself. A few days after the project was done, she texted me: "Adam, I just wanted to thank you again for this project. It came at a time when I really needed it. I'm so grateful to have met you and to have this project spread some love and light in my life and in others."[10]

Adventure. It might seem normal to some, but I'd argue that every adventure God sends us on is supernatural.

Jesus went on a lot of adventures that were clearly supernatural. Giving sight to the blind. Healing the sick. Blessing people who couldn't walk with the ability to do so.

But there were many other things Jesus did that seemed quite simple and pretty ordinary. Touching the leper who hadn't been touched by another person in a long time. Standing with the lady caught in adultery when everyone else was grabbing stones. Taking the time to listen to the two blind men everyone else was telling to be quiet. For me, the times I've most clearly seen God's love have been through people. Through Jake. Joy. Antonio. Tyler and Travis. A neighbor named Laurent. Brett. Rick and Val. My kids. My wife.

Sure, adventure can show us a ton about God's love and the way we're called to love others, but it's when I see God's love in the person looking back at me that love begins to have a name.

Jerry.

Remember my makeshift desk on the street corner? At first, all I got were a lot of puzzled looks as people walked past and stared at my "Need to talk? Pull up a chair" sign. I was pretty discouraged. *This was a bad idea!* I thought. I was increasingly sure that no one would stop. I mean, who would?

But I was wrong. After a while, people began to talk to me, thanking me for being open to listening to them as they walked past.

"What would you talk with me about?" one guy asked.

"Whatever *you'd* want to talk about," I said.

"You mean you really just want to listen to people?"

"Yep. I just want to listen."

"That's so kind of you. Thank you for loving people."

In between people stopping by, I worked at writing this chapter, until I looked up and saw a man standing next to my desk. I'd guess he was sixty years old or so, a sharp, professional-looking guy.

"So, I can just sit in this chair?" he asked.

"Yep."

"All right. Well, my name is Jerry. I'm just waiting till my son gets off from work. Life has just been really stressful lately. But I was enjoying walking around downtown here."

He then went on to share about his job as a chemist. For ten minutes or so, he talked about his job and all that he loved about it, mostly using a bunch of academic words I didn't understand. With pride and excitement, he shared about his past accomplishments and how proud he was of the son he was waiting for.

I listened and said it was good to hear about his family and job. "It's none of my business, but earlier you mentioned you were stressed. Please don't feel any pressure to share, but do you want to talk about that?" I asked.

"Well . . ." he began and then started crying. Sobbing uncontrollably. Because he was wearing sunglasses, I couldn't see his eyes, but the tears were streaming down his face.

"I'm so sorry. This is embarrassing," he said.

"Don't be sorry or embarrassed. I'm so glad I can sit with you."

He continued to sob. "Lately I've been struggling with so much anxiety," he said. "I've been having panic attacks. I'm so sorry."

"Please, don't be sorry. I've struggled with anxiety myself. I'm so glad I can listen."

"I saw your sign when I walked past earlier. And I decided that if you were still here when I got back, I would sit down. Thank you for listening."

"I'm honored to do so." I went on to tell him not to be embarrassed, that it might be wise to talk with a professional counselor about his anxiety, and that I go to see a counselor myself.

I said, "I don't know where you are or what you believe, but have you ever thought about inviting God into your darkness? Invite him into your anxiety, your hurt, into all the stress and things you're trying to process."

He started sobbing again. After regaining his composure, he pointed to himself and quietly asked, "You think God would want to be part of this mess?"

"I have no doubt. Even in the darkest valley, God is with us. Jesus is close to us in our hurt and in our pain, and he'd be so honored to enter into this with you."

As he listened to my words, the man continued to cry. He sat with me for close to an hour, and by the time 5 p.m. rolled around, it was time for him to go meet his son. He got up to leave and turned around, looking like he'd forgotten something. "Can I ask what your name is?"

"It's Adam," I said. "And you've just made my day."[11]

• • •

Ted the neighbor kid. The kids at Ambrase Lekol. Jillian. Jerry. I'm smiling just thinking about each of these people. They're people I wouldn't have met if I'd followed my five-year plan or my agenda for the day.

Following Jesus is an adventure. You never know where you'll end up or, better yet, who you'll meet. What if our agendas were about people? About names? About stories? Maybe then our agendas would look more like God's adventure.

Love opens us up to adventures. Love opens us to people and their names and stories. Without love, we stay closed off. Without love, our agendas matter more. But love pushes us outside the walls of our agendas and into the adventures God has in store for us.

Love makes every day an adventure.

PART 3

Your Name

God loves each of us as if there were only one of us.

—Saint Augustine

21

You

The one Jesus loves.

At my parents' house, there's a magnifying mirror attached to a wall by their bathroom sink. It's a small, circular mirror that you can pull out to get it super close to your face. I think the mirror is just a sign that my parents are getting older, but each time I'm at their house, I find myself pulling the mirror out to look at my face anyway.

You can see everything in that mirror! Every square millimeter of real estate on my face. I'd like to say that I stand there in awe of how beautifully and wonderfully made my face is, but the opposite is actually true.

In that magnifying mirror, I notice each and every ear hair.

I see every pimple in the making.

Random imperfections that I never noticed on my chin seem so huge that I wonder why no one ever pointed them out to me.

It's horrible. I leave my parents' bathroom slightly depressed each time.

Why is it that we often only notice our flaws?

• • •

This book is full of people who have taught me how to love. I've learned so much from each person, each name, and each story. Some were easy to love, and some were not so easy. But nobody is more difficult to love than the person in the mirror—me.

Yeah, you read that right. The hardest person for me to love is *myself,* no question.

I'm critical of myself. I give a lot of truth and very little grace. Even after some kind of success, I'm quick to point out my flaws and how I could have done it better. I'm always looking for growth areas. I struggle to receive a compliment.[1]

Looking back on my thirty-eight years of life, I can no doubt see a lot of positives—things I've done, goals I've accomplished—but I can also spot my regrets. Like the imperfections on my chin in that mirror, my regrets seem much bigger than any of the positives.

Failures.

Mistakes.

Words I want to take back.

Actions that I wish took place only in a dream, not real life.

Even after following Jesus for twenty years, there are still parts of my life that are broken.

A few weeks ago, I didn't use my words well. I was in a meeting with the team that works closest with me, and I was getting impatient. They weren't understanding what I was trying to say, and I kept growing more and more frustrated as time went on. I didn't yell, call names, or do anything crazy, but I did regret my impatient, short words, especially with a crew of people who have been so patient and grace filled with me.

Later that night, after Bec and I had both gotten into bed, we turned our lights off and I turned on my fan, something I do every night. As we lay there in silence, just the fan blowing, she could tell something was up with me. "What?" was all she asked. The only words I could get out were "Sometimes I still just feel so broken."

Yes, I struggle with loving myself, but I also struggle with receiving love from others. I worry that if people discover the real me, they'll see the broken, imperfect person I am and walk out of my life, no questions asked. But most of all, I struggle to understand God's love for me.

As clearly as I can see my ear hairs in that magnifying mirror, I see all the ugliness in my life, and I wonder how Jesus could love me. I know what my life *really* looks like. I see each and every imperfection.

Harsh words spoken.

Moments of impatience where I did yell, call names, or freak out.

Ugly things I've thought about people.

Epic parenting fails. (Did I really act completely insane in my back-yard in front of my kids?)

Hidden motives that weren't good.

Things in my past that I regret big-time.

Seasons when I didn't love my family well.

When my life is magnified, all the things I try so hard to hide and smooth over in front of others appear huge to a God I can't hide from. With those things front and center, I regularly question how a perfect God could ever love that person in the mirror looking back at me.

• • •

One of Jesus's closest friends was a guy named John. John was a fisherman, the son of a dude named Zebedee.[2] John was one of the first people to follow Jesus and would often refer to himself as "the one whom Jesus loved."[3] If you're a person who doesn't struggle in the self-confidence area, you're like John, the opposite of me. *The one Jesus loves? Really? That's a pretty bold statement, John!*

Looking at the remainder of John's life, though, this love was the real deal, and it would lead John to spread the gospel all over the world until he died an old man.[4] John didn't just talk about God's love for him—he lived in it. It was his identity.

Yeah, I'm a fisherman.

Yeah, my dad is a guy with the great name Zebedee.

But who am I? I'm the one Jesus loves!

As for me, I regularly base my identity off things other than Jesus. Yes, I often base it off good things like my wife and my four hooligans, but more often than not, I'm quick to define myself based on things like my job and how I'm doing at work on any given day. To define myself based on what others think of me or how many people validate me within a day with likes, comments, smiles, messages, or compliments.

Years ago, the great Henri Nouwen shared the five lies we tell ourselves about our identity:[5]

1. I am what I have.
2. I am what I do.
3. I am what other people say or think of me.
4. I am nothing more than my worst moment.
5. I am nothing less than my best moment.

At one point or another, I've believed each of these five lies. Heck, within the span of any given *day,* I catch myself believing these lies, sometimes several at the same time. When we let our lives become defined by any of these, it leads us to search for worth in areas where we were never meant to find it—and then become devastated when things, people, or circumstances change. Even if we find our worth in good things like our marriages, kids, or jobs, our identities are uncertain and fragile.

I recently had an older man share with me that it was only when he retired and no longer had a job that he realized how much of his identity and world were wrapped up in his career. A confident man for years, he found himself scrambling to figure out his worth months into retirement. You could see the uncertainty in his eyes.

But being "the one Jesus loves"—I want that! I want an identity that's unchanging, that's constant and forever the same.

No matter what the public opinion is.

No matter how ugly my words or actions were.

No matter my success or failure.

No matter what others say or secretly think about me.

No matter if my kids move out and go to college, or I retire after years of working the same job.

The one Jesus loves.

Luckily for us, John wrote a few letters that tell us more about being the one Jesus loves.[6] In one of them, John shares all about love—being loved by God and loving others.

John tells us, "Real love is Jesus giving his life for us."[7]

If we grew up in the church, we've maybe heard this verse before, but John didn't learn about this kind of love in Sunday school. Instead, he knew this kind of love from firsthand experience, from literally and physically being with Jesus.

He learned it from the God that so loved the world that he sent Jesus.

Jesus, the one who gives eternal life to anyone who believes in him.[8]

Jesus, the friend John got to sit with and listen to.

Jesus, who John physically traveled and ate with.

Jesus, who John slept near and talked with.

Jesus, John's perfect friend who died on a cross for everyone, starting with the two criminals who hung next him, along with the Roman guards who literally nailed him to that cross.

This God, this Jesus—he loved unconditionally. Without any asterisks or exceptions.

He loved people like John.

Like Trevon.

Tony.

Antonio.

Joy.

Mark.

A. C. Kidd.

Brett.

Rick and Val.

Shirley.

Me.

You.

Do you know that you're loved by God? That God sent Jesus for you? He sent Jesus to find you when you feel lost. To put you back together when you're broken. To be the center and basis of who you are.

Jesus knows your name. Yes, yours. He knows your story. All of it. And he loves you so much. With complete grace and truth.

As a matter of fact, you are the one Jesus loves. And so am I.

* * *

Some of my earliest memories as a kid revolve around church and God. My family attended church every single week! Unless someone was near death or we were on one of our very few family vacations, the Webers *never* missed church.

They're not positive church memories, though.[9] Instead, they're memories of weekly trying to convince my parents that I was sick and shouldn't go to church.[10] Memories of mocking the pastor during the services as he led recited prayers.[11] Memories of mindlessly counting the number of lights on our church's sanctuary ceiling. Memories of being so relieved when the hour of torture we called church was over. I didn't believe in God, and I hated going to church. These are the memories I have as a seven- and eight-year-old kid.

As I got older, my doubts and dislike for all things related to God only continued to grow. I was about the most laid-back, easygoing person you could meet—unless God came up in conversation. In high school, I once was invited by a close friend to a Bible study and snapped at him, "Are you nuts? We made it through confirmation already. Why would I ever go to more than the Sunday morning services my parents force me to go to? Please don't ever ask me to go to that again!"

In an English class one day, someone brought up God, and I quickly blurted out, "You'd have to be an idiot to believe in Jesus!" These are my memories as a sophomore in high school.

Later in my sophomore year, my family switched churches. I thought it was a terrible idea. Yet walking into the new church that first Sunday was so different from anything I had ever experienced before. People actually seemed like they wanted to be there.

What? You like church? You can't smile in church! Stop smiling. And stop clapping!

It didn't seem like the hour of torture by boredom I was used to. And the sights weren't so bad for a high school guy either—the new church was filled with cute girls my age.

Each Sunday, the pastor shared about Jesus. Instead of the words going over my head and sounding like gibberish or a bad history lesson at best, the words began to hit me right in the chest. This pastor wasn't a high-energy, charismatic preacher or anything. Instead, he was a simple, soft-spoken, kind man. During the messages, I would find myself getting emotional, and I couldn't explain why. It felt like he was talking directly to me and my family.

Is he digging through our trash or something? How does he know this about me?

Soon I began to quietly look forward to going to church and hearing what the pastor had to say. Slowly, something started to happen within me. I couldn't deny that there was something to this "God thing" that I had made fun of and looked down on for so long.

I wasn't looking for Jesus. I wasn't spiritual or even open to God. I wanted nothing to do with him—yet he wanted everything to do with me.

One particular Wednesday night, on my drive home from youth group, I arrived at the undeniable conclusion that God was real. I couldn't believe it—I was shocked by where I was. I remember audibly speaking the words, "God, you are who you say you are," but then the very next thing I thought was, *And there is no way you would want anything to do with me! Nothing!*

It was a sense of deep joy—*God, you are something I have unknowingly been searching for my whole life and now I've found you*—turning to grief—*How could you ever love me?*

I thought of all the years when I had spoken so poorly about God, mocked pastors, and been sarcastic when anyone even mentioned God or Jesus in front of me. In my head, if someone had made fun of me for years and then all of a sudden wanted to be my friend, I wouldn't have thought twice before saying, "What? Screw you!"

More than that, though, I knew the person in the mirror.

The curly-haired kid who struggled to fit in during elementary school.

The kid who tried so hard to earn the love of classmates but failed to do so.

The person who had a hard time receiving love from anyone because he was so sure that if someone truly got to know him she would reject him.

The person who never got too serious in dating relationships so he couldn't be rejected.

The person who constantly questioned his worth and lovableness.

The person who daily feels like a failure.

The person I am—my story, how many things I've messed up, how many things I wished I could take back.

Why would God want me? At the time, I was a high school kid who had all kinds of crap in his private life. How could God want me? I was so sure he wouldn't and didn't.

But on one particular Sunday, my pastor was speaking about the love of God, and he mentioned some words from this guy named John: "See what great love the Father has lavished on us."[12]

For the first time ever, my soul heard God whisper, *You are the one that I love, Adam.*

Over the years, this is still the single hardest thing for me to believe about God. Not God's existence. Not why evil exists in the world. Not why bad things happen to good people. Sure, I've asked and wrestled with these questions, but not nearly as much as I have with God's love.

At times, I've heard God say it loud and clear: *You are the one that I love.*

Other times, I know he's speaking the words, but I can't seem to hear them: *You are the one that I love.*

This statement goes completely against everything we're taught— that we need to earn someone's love. It goes completely against a lot of the things I'm constantly telling myself, such as, *You're not good enough. If people discover the real you, they'll walk away.*[13]

It goes against what I tell myself after screwing up: *There's no way God will love you after this!*

It goes against what the world tries to tell us, that love comes from success, from earning the attention and validation of others.

Although I would never rationally say that we need to earn God's love, I'm regularly guilty of living like that's true. Over the years, I've often strived to do enough for God. To do enough good things. To help enough people. To do enough religious things. To tell enough people about Jesus. To not do or even *think* about bad things. To succeed in enough ways for God. I keep running and running and running and—all the while God is speaking, *You are the one I love.*

It's this truth that's changed my life and my story, and I know it has the power to change yours too.

• • •

Being the one Jesus loves is great and all, but how do we actually begin to *feel* his love in our lives? How do we move this from a nice Sunday-school answer to our hearts—to understand it the same way John did? How do we let it change us from the inside out—changing how we think of ourselves, how we think of other people, and who we think Jesus is to us?

I'll be honest, it's easier said than done. Just like my experience with my parents' magnifying mirror, it's all too easy for us to spot our every flaw. Today, this feels more accurate than ever.

But the truth is, we—you and I—are the ones he loves, and embracing that love starts with understanding our stories. Some of us are lucky enough (or maybe not so lucky) to have big, flashy stories that garner us headlines and get us written into history books. If that's you, that's awesome! But most of us are probably more like Shirley, Joy, Brett, Rick and Val, Tyler and Travis—people whose stories may not be remembered by everyone but whose lives point to one thing: they are the ones whom Jesus loves.

Each of these people has used their story to serve and impact other people for Jesus—noticing the unnoticeable, multiplying generosity, comforting through the worst, staying when everyone else leaves. They've used their stories to make an impact.

You might be thinking, *That's great and all, Adam. I'm glad Rick and Val and Shirley and Joy have stories that have changed lives. But what about my story? My story isn't anything special, plus I still don't really believe that I'm the one Jesus loves.* No worries! Let's take a step back. As much as I can try to tell you that you are the one Jesus loves, this truth won't change anything about you or your story if you don't believe it yourself.

Just like the first step to loving others is knowing their stories, the first step to realizing and feeling the love God has for us is in knowing our own stories—the good, the bad, and the times when we saw God's love so clearly.

Go back and start at the beginning: What are some of the highlights of your life up to this point? Times when you felt encouraged, special, loved? On the flip side, what are the lowlights? What are the hard, horrible things you've experienced? What are the memories that you'll never forget, good and bad? How have the highlights and lowlights of your life affected the way you view and see the world? Now, how have you seen God at work through it all? When have you felt close to God? Are there times when you felt wonderful feelings— before you even believed in God—that you can't explain? Are their times when you were lifted out of a dark place you were in?

This doesn't have to be some cut-and-dried process of self-examination, either. Sure, you can write these things out in a notebook, putting them down on paper to clarify your thoughts, but mostly I'm just wanting you to talk with God. Take a bird's-eye view look at your life and look for the places where you've seen God at work. Like me, I'm sure you'll find some not-so-good moments, but I know without a doubt that memories of love, happiness, and warmth will come to the surface too.

Taking one step further, believing this truth that God loves us hinges on one thing: actually spending time with Jesus. Every day. I know, super exciting and life changing, right? Trust me, it is.

Believing you're the one Jesus loves starts with spending time with the one who loves you—Jesus. I'm not sure what that looks like for you, but for me it often looks like ten minutes at a quiet coffee shop in the mornings after my kids are dropped off at school, taking a little time to just be still. No emails, no checklists, nothing—just Jesus and my Bible. Being still and asking God to speak. Or writing out the things I'm worried and stressed about and asking him to carry them for me. Other times, it's worshipping in my car (singing at the top of my lungs) or sitting on my front porch listening to the wind blowing through my maple trees, in awe of God, the one who created all things. Spending time with Jesus could look a million different ways:

Taking a walk and just praying as you look up at the sky.

Journaling. Writing down your thoughts and prayer requests to God.

Reading a devotional in the morning or before bed.[14]

Setting a reminder on your phone to pray at certain times of the day.

Whatever it is, take the time to be with Jesus today. It's not just good for you (like eating your vegetables; thanks, Mom); it's key to believing and *knowing* in your soul that you're the one Jesus loves.

We're able to fully believe that we're the one Jesus loves only when we find our identities solely in this truth, not from anything or anyone else. What do I mean by "identity"? It's who you say you are. It's what you think is the most important thing about you. So, to figure out what you base your identity on, ask yourself some questions:

When I introduce myself, what are the first few things I tell other people or want them to know?

When am I most stressed? What am I specifically stressed about?

When I fail, how do I feel? What is the one thing in my life that I never want to fail at?

What are one or two things in life that I can't live without?

What is one thing I'm afraid people might find out about me?

Examine yourself. When you do, I'm certain you'll find some areas where you're placing your identity in something other than Jesus. I know I have. I have a list of things! We're human, after all.

Once you find the area or areas you're basing your identity on, take another step. Acknowledge it, to yourself and to Jesus.

This might look like telling a friend. And telling God about where you're placing your identity.

If possible, take a break from the area that you're quick to run to instead of Jesus.

Ask God to help you:

Jesus, I give this area to you. I hand over control of it.

I no longer want my worth, value, or identity to come from it.

I want my worth to come from you. From who you say I am.

I want my identity to be founded on the great love you have for me.

Whatever it is, do anything you can to find your identity in Jesus and only in him. When you do, I promise you'll begin, maybe for the first time, to understand that you—yes, you—are the one Jesus loves.

• • •

As I write this, in the place and season of life I'm in right now, God is speaking the loudest he ever has to me.

He's speaking words of encouragement to me: *You can do this, Adam. I'm so proud of you.*

Words of guidance: *Follow me today, Adam. My plan is easy, and my burden is light.*

Words of love: *You, Adam, with all your flaws, mistakes, and things you wish you could take back—you are the one I love.*

This isn't because God's voice has magically gotten louder for me. It's because my life and the things competing for his voice have gotten quieter. He's not speaking any louder; I'm just finally listening to him more.

• • •

My oldest son, Hudson, is a bit of a perfectionist. Scratch that—he's a complete perfectionist! He hates making mistakes. He hates looking foolish. He responds to an A- on a school project the same way I used to respond to a D+. Anything he does, he wants to do perfectly.

The other day I picked him up from school, and he was so excited to tell me he had made the jazz band at school. I quickly said, "That's wonderful, Hudson! So awesome!" He had been practicing daily for months and was over-the-moon excited, and I was over-the-moon excited for him.

Moments later, after the celebration died down a bit, I felt God nudging me to speak. We stopped at a red light, and I looked over at Hudson, staring directly in his eyes. I wanted his soul to hear my words.

"Hudson, I'm so proud of you for trying so hard at something you love. It's so exciting you made the jazz band. But I just want you to know:

That on your worst day.

After your biggest failure.

Your greatest embarrassment.

At your lowest moment.

When everyone else is walking away from you. I'll still be by your side.

I'll still be cheering you on.

I'll still be proud of you.

Even then, I'll still love you."

With his eyes focused on mine, you could see the words warm his heart. It was almost like his soul had taken a breath.

On an infinitely greater level, this is God's love for us.

He looks us in the eyes, and gently speaks the words.

Even then, I'll still love you.

Even then, I'll still love you, Adam.

Even then, I'll still love you, (your name).

You are the one Jesus loves.

To God, this isn't just another title of ours. It's not another detail about us. It's not a part of our identity. In his eyes, it's *who we are.*

You are the one Jesus loves, and so am I.

He loves you.

It's not just something he does, *it's who he is.*

It's his name.

Jesus.

Though our feelings come and go, His love for us does not.

—Clive Staples Lewis

Thank you.

To pastors, friends, and the wonderful people who have poured into me: Roger and Joan Spahr, Brad Lomenick, Bishop Ough, Matt Brown, Luke and Lindsey Lezon, Jon Weece, Ken Costa, Tyler Reagin, Jason Laird, David Calhoun, C. J. and Stephanie Ham, Chris Brown, Michael Schlact, Juli Wilson, Heidi Shives, Anthony and Kendra Siemonsma, Stephanie Keyes, John and Kaylee Koch, Dave DeVries, Aaron Pennington, Jael Thorpe, Rob Wilton, Mark Sayers, Joel Bennett, Paul TenHaken, Travis Jacobs, Melissa Goff, Trevor Ferguson, Justin Lathrop, Carlos Whittaker, Brian and Andrea Rock, Austin and Calli Walker, Jessie Finke, Jess Waltner, Justin and Kristin Nichols, Rashawn Copeland, Daniel Fusco, Jim Lake, Mike Foster, Jennifer Dukes Lee, Scott Sauls, Andy Dalton, Shannen Bozied, Jason Roy, Josh Gagnon, Casey Helmick, Nick and Bekah Hauert, Dustin Strande, Jered and Callie Schock, Stuart Norberg, Carey Nieuwhof, Chad and Sarah Kurtenbach, Reid and Lauren Vander-Veen, Kristopher and Rachel Gage, Phill Tague, Paul Marzahn, Jason Strand, Ryan Konz, Steve Martyn, Rex and Julie Benz, Gary and Chris Haugan, John with all the old cool stuff in your garage, Eric and Jessica Rice, Matt Best, Jerrid Sebesta, Ben and Ashley Statema, Brooks and Leah Pidde, Darrin Patrick, Lisa Whittle, Hal Donaldson, Dan Dykhouse, Tara Rollinger, Jason Romano, Nike Ohonme, Ben Ingebretson, Tom Patterson, Kevin Smith, James JB Brown, Lisa Bevere, Brad Montague, Mark Batterson, Kait Warman, Jeff Henderson, Jay and Katherine Wolf, Adam Hamilton, JD Walt, Nicole Zasowski, Jeremy DeWeerdt, Ryan Romeo, Joe Hubers, Chris Durso, Denisse Copeland, Rebecca Trefz, Dwight, Jay Huizenga, and so many more.

To my siblings: Hugh and Amy Weber, Luke Weber, and Becca and Seth Honeyman. I love each of you.

To everyone who helped shape this book in any way: Kaylyn Mehlhaff, Travis Waltner, Patty Crowley, Danielle Ferguson, Jason Smith, Kylee Breems, Rick Post, Wendy Tryon, Rick Melmer, and Rachel Dewey.

To Andrew Stoddard, Paul Pastor, Douglas Mann, Helen Macdonald, and everyone at WaterBrook, I'm so grateful that I get to work with one of the best publishers there is.

To Chris Ferebee, I still can't believe that you took a chance on me.

To Angela Scheff, I'm forever thankful for your constant encouragement and guidance. I pinch myself after each time we talk.

To Tim Willard, thanks for seeing something in me that I didn't see in myself. Thank you for opening doors for me that I could have never opened alone. This book and any future books are because of you.

To Embrace Church, thank you for being my family, my team, and my friends. Thank you for the honor of allowing me to be your pastor.

To Kaylyn Mehlhaff, your fingerprints are all over this book, helping these stories and chapters to come alive and come together. It's been an absolute joy and honor to see you grow as an editor through this book. Anyone need a book editor? Kaylyn is one of the best!

To my closest friends who have carried me to Jesus for the past couple of years: Tyler Goff, Travis Waltner, Rick Post, Cody Bozied, Holly Brown, Jason Smith, Rick and Val Melmer, Matt LeRoy, Jarrid Wilson, Travis Finke, Troy Keyes, Matt Tobin, Ben Shives, Brian Thorpe, and so many more. Instead of walking away from me, you got closer. I'll never be able to thank you enough.

To Mom and Dad, Jim and Nancy Weber, I love you both. I thank God for each day and every year I have with you.

To Hudson, Wilson, Grayson, and Anderson, you show me Jesus daily, and I only hope I do the same for you. I love being your dad more than words can explain. Love you.

To Bec, thank you for choosing to love me each day. You're my best friend, my biggest cheerleader, and my wife. I love you. So much. Your book is next.

To each person who let me share their story, your story has impacted mine and countless others. I know it'll impact the life of each person who reads this book.

To you, the reader, I'm humbled that you'd read anything I write. I only hope that this book would help you understand how to love others. More than that, I hope it'd help you understand the deep love that Jesus has for you.

To you, Jesus, for finding me when I was lost, for putting me back together when I was broken, for defending me when I couldn't defend myself. For being my friend, savior, and Lord.

Field notes.

Dedication

1. When it comes to someone who loved well, Jarrid Wilson was the best. Do you struggle with mental health or love someone who does? You are loved. Find hope at www.anthemofhope.org.

Introduction

1. In college, my friend Wipes drove a 1984 Ford Econoline van. He put in a stick shift, along with a full-length couch in the back. Shadiest van ever! Some of the greatest memories of my life (and some of my mom's worst memories!) are of the road trips Wipes and I took in this van. My mom was convinced I would end up dead or in prison somehow. On one of our road trips, Wipes and I drove 5,300 miles in five days, hitting twenty-six states. We also saw every major tourist attraction this wonderful country has to offer: the groundhog in Punxsutawney, Pennsylvania; Minnesota's Largest Candy Store; the Chattahoochee River, while listening to Alan Jackson—all the major stops!

2. There are few things that I would enjoy more than hearing from you. Have a question about something? Wish there was a field note about something I didn't explain? Do you like randomly posting pictures online of books you're reading? Tag me. Tweet me. Message me. @adamaweber on Instagram. @adamweber on Twitter. I would be thrilled to hear from you!

3. A quick history lesson: At this time, the Jewish people listening to Jesus had somewhere in the range of 613 commandments. There were specific commandments on everything: What to eat

and what not to eat. Specific rules on how to please and worship God. Rules on not gossiping, how to cut your hair, even
farming. You name it, they had a rule for it. Sadly, Christians
today aren't much different. You need to do this and not do that.
If you're a good Christian, you need to be really holy and do a lot
of religious, churchy things. People will know how much you love
God by your theology, church attendance, and how well you
keep the rules. Yet Jesus tells us all the commandments are
summed up in two commands: loving God and loving others
(see Matthew 22:37–40). Basically, Jesus is keeping it really
simple. He's asking, *Do you want to please me? Do you want
to follow me? Then love me and love people. You want to really
be like me? Then really love me and really love others.*

1 | Jesus

1. I started a church called Embrace in Sioux Falls, South Dakota,
    when I was twenty-four years old. At the first service, back in Sep-
    tember of 2006, we had thirty-two people show up. Now each
    week, we have a few more people than that and they come to
    several different campuses. I never imagined what this church
    would become. I never wanted to be a pastor, but I'm so glad I fol-
    lowed God's plan instead of mine. #Godsplan #Drake. Embrace
    is going to come up several times in this book, so I thought I'd give
    you a heads-up right from the get-go.
2. Chandler Harris, that's a moment I'll never forget! By the way,
    you have the best parents ever.
3. Go follow the Twitter account @HoodJesusYo if you're not
    already doing so.
4. A man from New York tried to sell on eBay a piece of toast that
    appeared to have the face of Jesus for $25,000! See Czarina
    Ong, "Man Trying to Sell His 'Jesus Toast' on eBay for $25K,"
    Christian Today, March 7, 2017, www.christiantoday.com/article
    /man-trying-to-sell-his-jesus-toast-on-ebay-for-25k/105294.htm.
    Grilled Cheesus! I now check my toast daily for images.
5. One night when my wife, Bec, and I first started dating, we got
    into a slight argument (aka fight) because I never introduced her
    to anyone. She thought I didn't care about her or want to intro-
    duce her to my classmates and friends. I told her it was the

complete opposite. I wanted to introduce her, but I didn't know anyone's name! Side note to you: please don't ever ask me if I know your name!

6. Tip: Facebook is the greatest wingman ever!

7. I would honestly love this. My wife, on the other hand? She avoids name tags like the plague.

8. To be clear, he knows the names of the people verified on Instagram and loves them as well. We often forget these people are people too—often broken and lonely people. Don't treat someone poorly just because they're well known or "famous."

9. This story comes from the book of Luke in the Bible. See Luke 19:1–10, which I've paraphrased. Throughout each chapter in this book, I'll be referencing stories found in the Bible quite a bit. If you've never picked up a Bible before, I'd encourage you to do so. I'll do my best to explain things in a way that anyone can understand.

10. If you know the words to the song, start singing! If you don't know the words, you didn't have a childhood. Search for "Zacchaeus Was a Wee Little Man" and watch the video. Seven hundred times! You can thank me later because you just got your childhood back. Unfortunately, this song will now be stuck in your head for the next seven hundred days.

11. This story about Nathanael and Jesus is from John 1:43–50, which I've paraphrased. Again, I would encourage you to take a moment, open up your Bible, and read the whole story. If this is something new for you, know I'm praying for you. That each story would come alive. That it would make sense. That it would meet you right where you are.

12. I struggled with what name to pick here. LeBron James, Beyoncé, Boomer Esiason.

13. I try and see grumpy people as a challenge. I'm going to try and love them so fully, genuinely, and almost annoyingly that even the hardest heart will begin to soften. This challenge hasn't backfired on me yet. No black eyes or anything.

14. John 1:14, NIV.

15. Thank God we don't have to kill sheep in church today. I like sheep. I only wish I could get some Gotland sheep for my backyard.

16. 1 John 4:8.
17. 1 John 4:10, paraphrased.
18. 1 John 4:20–21, paraphrased.
19. If our love of God doesn't result in us loving others, we're not loving God. That's hard for some of us to grasp.
20. The field notes are my personal favorite part of the book!

2 | Jake

1. Looking back, Girbaud jeans are actually pretty ugly. Why would you want to put a tag near your zipper and highlight that area?

2. Don't know Ickey Woods? Go search for "The Ickey Shuffle" on Google. You'll be better for it.

3. Jake (the chicken) was such a great chicken. A white leghorn. He'd walk down the driveway with me to get the mail. That is, until he got killed by a weasel one night. That was the end of Jake the chicken. Did I mention that I also grew up having a goat, a donkey, a pig with a bad leg, lots of geese, and peacocks? No, we didn't live at the zoo. One day the peacocks accidentally got out of their pen, and for two straight years, they slept on the roof of our house and crowed every morning. Ever heard a peacock crow? Loudest, most annoying bird ever!

4. Deb Schlueter, thanks for being so good to my mom over the years. I thank God for you and Gene.

5. My glasses were brown and thick rimmed. Looking back at some of my elementary-school pictures and seeing those glasses and some of the clothes I wore, I question if my parents really loved me. Ha! One day in second grade, my glasses broke because a bigger kid fell on me. My dad picked me up from school to go to the eye doctor for a new pair of glasses. The only pair they could get me that day were ones with Mickey Mouse on both sides of the frames. I was horrified, and my dad could clearly tell. Thankfully, he had a plan. Before dropping

me back off at school, we stopped by our house and he took a metal grinder to my glasses, cutting off Mickey. When I got back to school, my glasses looked like they had gone through a metal grinder (because they had), but at least I had my pride.

6. If you haven't noticed, the guy on the back of the book is really bald! And has been for quite some time. Why, God?

7. My favorite school-bus driver was nicknamed "Bruce the Moose."

8. My last day of sixth grade, I walked from Milbank Middle School to my Grandma Dahle's house. Once there, I hopped in the car with my family and we drove to Clark. I was literally the last thing to be packed and moved.

9. Bergsaker Hall second floor, at Augustana College. It's now called Augustana University and it's pretty much the Harvard of South Dakota.

10. Fun fact: for my first book signing at Barnes & Noble, Jake showed up. I hadn't seen him in years. I couldn't believe it, yet in the same breath, it didn't surprise me. That's Jake!

11. Looking back at your life, are there people you need to thank? Someone who made you feel loved when you really needed it? A neighbor who showed you kindness? A teacher who encouraged you to dream big? I'd be so grateful if you'd call them, grab coffee with them, or write them a letter to say thank you!

12. Is it strange that I actually look forward to meeting with my tax guy every year? Pat Azzara, I'm sure I'll see you soon.

13. This story about Levi and Jesus is from Mark 2:13–17, which I've paraphrased.

3 | Joy

1. My dad was trained as an electrician under a woman named Goldie.

2. The hardware store Dad bought was called Coast to Coast. It was a hard season financially, but it was wonderful in a lot of ways. My mom and dad got to work closely with each other in the store. My brother Luke and I would often drive our family golf cart from our house on the edge of Clark to the hardware store to see Mom and Dad, grab a pop and maybe a box of shotgun shells to go hunting later. It was small-town South Dakota at its best. I thank God for the years we lived in Clark, South Dakota.

3. If you ever need a home in Watertown, South Dakota, look up Haugan Nelson Realty, run by two of the most wonderful women you'll ever meet.

4. Joy has already willed her home and the entire ranch away to a church so that it will remain a camp and retreat center for kids and adults long after she's no longer walking around the ranch. It's just another testament to a life spent joyfully giving what she has to help others.

5. I can't even begin to list all of the people like Joy who have been generous to me and my family and as a result have made me want to be more generous. I think of the people at Tolstoy United Methodist Church, a church I've never been to, who sent Bec and me a check every single month to help us pay for seminary. I think of Rex and Julie who generously restored my family's tractor for me without me asking. I think of a friend who stopped by the church one day with a check for $100,000. While I'm sure that friend does well, I know he's not rich. I think of people like Brad Lomenick and Matt Brown who have generously opened doors and introduced me to people I would have never met otherwise. I could go on and on and on.

6. The story about the young boy's lunch and Jesus is from Matthew 14:13–21 and John 6:1–15, which I've paraphrased.

7. My favorite David Copperfield show is the time he made an entire train disappear. I'm still trying to figure out where that train went.

8. I always get a little scared when my wife gets hangry! Love you, Bec.

9. I was in accelerated math throughout middle school and did well in high school. At the start of my freshman year of college, I asked my advisor if I could take calculus. She told me that it would probably be better if I didn't take it the first semester. I told her I was good at math and wasn't concerned. Well, I should have been. I've never worked harder in a class in my life. I even got help from a tutor and was still only pulling a D+ by the end of the semester. The last day of class my calculus professor said, "Adam, you've worked so hard. I'm giving you a C-." A C- was all I needed for my major. I'm not sure if he was being

generous or if he just didn't want me in his class for another semester. Either way, I chalk it up to a miracle!

10. Exodus 16:20. We struggle to listen to God's instructions, and so did the Israelites.

11. The deep philosopher Puff Daddy with The Notorious B.I.G. and Mase has a song titled, "Mo Money Mo Problems" (*Life After Death,* Bad Boy, 1997). This is still one of my favorite music videos.

12. When God lays something on your heart, go do it! Don't approach your church and ask them to do something. *You* are the church. Gather a few friends—if money is required, take some from your bank account and ask friends to do the same—and go do it! This is one of the greatest steps in discipleship that you can possibly take. Stop asking the church to do things, and become the church yourself!

13. See Acts 20:35.

14. Something we often forget to do is write down what we've given—not to brag or boast in it, but to go back months later to see how God has multiplied our generosity. It should leave us bragging about God, not ourselves. This simple act of looking back will only encourage us to give more.

4 | Antonio

1. For some unknown reason, we have random flies that live in the sanctuary that I preach live from. It can be forty below outside in the middle of the winter, yet we still have flies. These flies also love to come out of hiding while I'm preaching in front of a whole bunch of people. Picture large flies buzzing around my head and dive-bombing my notes as I'm preaching. #getbehindmeSatan

2. Between you and me, right before I preach, I always check to make sure the zipper on my pants is up. Strange but true. Would there be anything worse than having everyone laugh because my zipper was down in front of the *entire* church?

3. Justin Bieber and I are tight. I can always dream.

4. This story about Mary and Jesus is in Luke 7:36–50, which I've paraphrased.

5. Rahab is another person in the Bible who was a prostitute. I'm

so thankful we're told these kinds of details. Oftentimes in church we dance around talking about things like sex, pornography, depression, suicide, addiction, and so on because we think it's not right to talk about them in church. Yet I'm so thankful we have Jesus, who isn't afraid to speak with us in our lowest and dirtiest places. I pray churches would become the first places to talk about these things, not the last. The lady speaking with Jesus was a woman who was paid for having sex. Maybe some of the men who were hanging around Jesus in this story were ones who went to her. There's no other way around it. Disgusting, right? Dirty. Embarrassing.

Have a place in your life that's pretty dirty or even disgusting? Even if it's not right to talk about in your specific church, Jesus would love to talk with you about it. Let him in.

6. See Matthew 26:13.

7. Answer this question to get a good gauge of your walk with Christ: How do you respond to "interruptions" throughout your day? Are you annoyed? Quick tempered? Many of the miracles we see in the Bible took place as a result of an interruption to Jesus's schedule. Next time you're interrupted, look to love—or even further, think about how you can provide a mini-miracle to someone. Lord, give us your heart.

8. See Genesis 1:27.

9. See Psalm 139:14, NIV.

5 | Tyler and Travis

1. Oddly enough, I can still remember where I called Tyler from: our apartment in Bettie Morrison Hall on the campus of Asbury Seminary. I remember it mainly because it didn't strike me as odd that I would call Tyler (who I barely knew) until I got off the phone with him.

2. They're impossible to miss! Also, Tyler and the mayor of Sioux Falls might be the two best-looking dudes in town.

3. I share more about this season in my book *Talking with God* (Colorado Springs, CO: WaterBrook, 2018).

4. Travis is the campus pastor at our Tea Campus in Tea, South Dakota. He started out as our executive pastor.

5. If you're a leader of any kind, you'll have to make hard decisions

like this. A leader in your home, team, business, nonprofit, or even friend group. Decisions you'll lose sleep over, but you know are the right decisions to make. Lord, give us courage. Everything looks easy as an armchair quarterback. Those who are doing very little will always shout the loudest. It is very easy to criticize others when you've never been criticized because you haven't done much worth criticizing. During this hard season in the church, I had countless leaders come up to me and tell me, "Keep your head up. You're a good man. Keep going!" Words I'll be forever grateful for. If you're in one of these seasons yourself, "Keep your head up. Keep going!" I'm praying for you! You're not alone.

6. If you've been hurt or jaded because of the church—any church— I'm so sorry! I now fully understand why so many people outside the church want nothing to do with it. My encouragement: give the church another chance. Like any family, it's messed up at times. But you and I need it.

7. Don't take my word for it—smart people from Harvard said it! See "The Health Benefits of Strong Relationships," *Harvard Women's Health Watch,* updated August 6, 2019, www.health .harvard.edu/newsletter_article/the-health-benefits-of-strong -relationships.

8. I also need to thank people like Rick Post, Cody Bozied, Jason Smith, Holly Brown, Matt LeRoy, and Travis Finke.

9. This story about the five friends and Jesus is from Mark 2:1–12, which I've paraphrased.

10. Even if you live a thousand miles from Sioux Falls, go follow @Argus911 on Twitter and Instagram. @Argus911 did a story once on a few people who cut a hole in the roof of a bar to steal an ATM. I still don't know how they did it, logistically. They stole the *entire ATM.* Granted, not a Jesus miracle, but it is a little Sioux Falls oddity.

11. If you have these friends, make sure to thank them. Tell them you love them. Make their friendship a priority. Carry them when they can't walk!

12. If you don't have friends like this but want them, pray for them! Pray that you would find close friends to walk through life with. Ask God for them. Also, put yourself out there. Invite a coworker

to lunch. Invite a family over to your house to enjoy a firepit and s'mores. If they say no, invite someone else! Also, if you get invited to something, show up. Don't flake out. Don't always be "too busy." Make time for the things that matter to you!

13. There are still things from this season that I don't fully understand, but I can honestly say now that so much good has come from it. I pray I never have to experience anything like it again, but I can thank God for the ways he grew me through it.

6 | Laurent

1. Live in Sioux Falls and like old houses? Move to the Cathedral District! It's so much better than McKennan Park. Just sayin'.

2. "A couple of others" means seven maple trees total. And I just planted two more oak trees. I know, I have a problem.

3. Every month or so in the summer, the kids and I will walk around our block with garbage bags and a wagon to pick up trash. We've met neighbors we would have never met otherwise. It gets the kids' hands dirty in a good way. I always remind the kids that we're not doing it because we're better than anyone. It's just something we can do. It's our own simple way to serve and care for our neighbors and the block we live on. And, honestly, it's really good for the soul. Our pride doesn't like doing things like this, but it reminds us that nothing is beneath us.

4. This story about the woman caught in adultery and Jesus is from John 8:1–11, which I've paraphrased.

5. Casual move. I only wish we knew what Jesus wrote in the sand that day.

6. Unless you treat your brothers and sisters poorly!

7 | Brett

1. Remember, we live in South Dakota. There's not many people, and most of us are cousins.

2. I've ridden on a horse only one time. I rode one out at Lost Valley Ranch in Colorado. Unfortunately, God didn't design my body to ride a horse. I'm not very flexible, and I struggled to get my legs around the horse. A cowboy named Bobby needed to lift me off the horse like you do a one-year-old out of a high chair. One of

the most humbling moments of my life. I'm still sore two years later. Thanks for lifting me off though, Bobby.

3. Recently, Brett told me that he had completed a DNA kit in the hopes of finding out more information about his background. Through a family match on ancestry.com, Brett found out who his biological father is. Nervously, he reached out to him. When Brett messaged me the news that he had found his biological father, he included a picture. The resemblance was so strong that at first I thought Brett was joking with me—something that wouldn't be a surprise if you know Brett. Minus the fact that Brett has cerebral palsy, the two are almost identical twins. Brett and his biological father have now connected and formed a relationship. Two months after he met his biological father, Brett was contacted and had the opportunity to meet his biological mother. They also now keep in contact. I never cease to be amazed by this journey that we call life.

4. Brett graduated from Southwest Minnesota State with a degree in therapeutic recreation. He has played able-bodied softball, wheelchair softball, wheelchair tennis, power soccer (power-wheelchair soccer), power hockey (power-wheelchair hockey), and sled hockey (wheelchair hockey on ice).

5. If you ever swing through Sioux Falls, Josiah's is a must stop. Great coffee and even better breakfast. The building was flipped a year or so ago, and now it's hard to believe the restaurant was a nasty transmission shop not too long ago. Not many people randomly "swing through Sioux Falls," but for the one person reading this who does, you're welcome!

6. Luke 23:53, NIV.

8 | Rick and Val

1. I went to prom with Tara one year. I think my hair was bigger than hers. For some strange reason, I went through a season of growing my hair out like a large bush on my head. Every time I see a picture of that prom, I wonder why someone didn't love me enough to tell me to cut the shrubbery on top of my head!

2. Is it weird to daydream about the heavenly body I'll have someday? A full head of hair and skin that tans to a beautiful golden-

brown color. I'll be able to run like a gazelle, and there won't even be a need for a washing machine in my house—my washboard abs will get the job done just fine.

3. Dakota Wesleyan University in Mitchell, South Dakota. Home of The World's Only Corn Palace. Who doesn't want a palace of corn in their town?

4. Bec's first job was working at Solomon's Porch in Wilmore, Kentucky. She also worked for an eye doctor named Doctor Ditto. Her last gig in Kentucky was working the front desk for the seminary. Her work phone number was easy to remember: 1-800-2-Asbury.

5. My favorite thing to purchase at a Kentucky grocery store? A six-pack of Ale-8-Ones in the tall glass bottles. So good. If you don't like it, keep drinking it until you do. It's an acquired, high-class drink.

6. During this time, instead of trying to share my side of the story with anyone who would listen, I really felt led to be quiet unless someone approached and asked me a question. If they asked, I would openly answer their questions. But if they didn't ask, I wouldn't say a word, even if I knew they had hard feelings toward me. Looking back, I'm so glad I took this approach. Zero regrets. God doesn't honor gossip, and he is a great defender!

7. Before becoming a pastor, I delivered flowers. I'll let you judge who had the better job between me and Paul.

8. 2 Corinthians 1:4.

9. 2 Corinthians 1:4, emphasis added.

10. Examples of prayers you might need to pray: *This sucks, God! Where are you? Why did I have to walk through hell like I did?* Too raw to pray? Not very Christian? You might want to read the Psalms again.

11. If you don't see a Christian counselor on a regular basis, you need to! Put it in your calendar. The worst that could happen is that you discover you're emotionally healthy—just like going to a regular checkup with a family doctor. "You're completely healthy!" Best news ever, right? I see a counselor once a month. At first I went kicking and screaming, but now it's a crucial part of my life as a husband, dad, pastor, friend, and human.

12. Someone is waiting (and needs) to hear your story. Yes, yours.

They're currently walking through the same trials you have, and they're waiting to be encouraged and comforted by your words.

13. Henri Nouwen was an amazing Catholic priest who died in 1996. He was a renowned author, teacher, and professor at academic institutions like Notre Dame, Yale Divinity School, and Harvard Divinity School until he decided to go off the grid and work at a special-needs facility for people with intellectual and developmental disabilities. See his book *The Wounded Healer: Ministry in Contemporary Society* (New York: Doubleday, 1972).

9 | Hudson, Wilson, Grayson, and Anderson

1. Hudson Ray: I thank God for how kind and caring you are. I love how you worship God on Sundays next to me and when we have "worship nights" together in the car. I can't wait to see the plans God has for you.

   Wilson Moses: I love how loyal and protective you are. I'm so glad that someone else in our family loves sports. One of my favorite memories is going to the SDSU versus NDSU football game together! Know you are loved so much.

   Grayson Marie: You're so much like your mom. Baby, I love cuddling with you, reading books with you, and telling you I love you from my car as you walk up to school, even though it drives you crazy!

   Anderson Adam: I love your energy and the passion you live each day with. I love going on tractor rides and being outside together. If you want to know what you'll look like in thirty years, just look at me!

2. If we ever have a fifth kid, I will cry for days. Maybe months. I'm still trying to figure out where kids come from.

3. Being a parent is the only job that can't be replaced. Bec could upgrade. Embrace could hire a new pastor. But I'll always be my kids' dad.

4. Pause here for a second. The house I hit was Bill's (my drug-dealing neighbor—you'll hear more about Bill in a later chapter). In the middle of my rampage, I did take a minute to thank God, thinking to myself, *Well, they're the last people on the planet who would call the cops about a shoe getting thrown at their house!* Thankfully, it wasn't my other neighbor; he's a finance

guy and probably wouldn't have taken a shoe hitting the side of his house so lightly. I love you, Brooks!

5. For the rest of their lives, my four kids will never let me forget the shoe-throwing incident. I wouldn't be surprised if a shoe is carved into the side of my gravestone someday.

6. This story about little children and Jesus is from Matthew 19:13–14, which I've paraphrased.

10 | Becky

1. I share all about how Bec and I met in my book *Talking with God* (Colorado Springs, CO: WaterBrook, 2017).

2. I've never loved you more, Bec.

3. We almost moved up the wedding date twice, but we had already sent out the invitations! Pro tip: the shorter your engagement, the better. You can thank me later.

4. I realize this is a privileged thought and isn't always the case. Some kids end up taking in parents, which is so honorable. Some siblings never marry and maybe live together or near one another. Sometimes kids can't afford to move out. Every situation is different.

5. Some of those things include chickens, old cars, tractor shows, typewriters, saltwater fish, old bridge lamps, water fountains, flowers. Please pray for my wife!

6. Are healthy marriages not the norm in your family? It won't be easy, but break the cycle by having a healthy marriage yourself.

7. This story about Jesus washing the disciples' feet is from John 13:1–17, which I've paraphrased.

8. Dr. Jay Moon, you're one of the best.

9. I have hair on every square inch of my body except where it's supposed to be. I only share this because I know you wanted to know.

11 | Trevon

1. *Gremlin* is actually the perfect way to describe my kids. One moment they're cute and cuddly, but add a little water (or sugar), and they can destroy your house and tear the whole city down. If you've seen the 1980s movie *Gremlins,* you know what I'm talking about!

2. Winter in South Dakota equals flesh-eating cold weather for months. We have two seasons here: winter and construction season.

3. Fifteen minutes is a long drive in South Dakota, especially considering that everyone here still rides horses.

4. This story about the religious man and Jesus is from Luke 10:25–37, which I've paraphrased.

5. The man gave the "right answer." He quoted the most important verses in the Jewish faith: the prayer referred to as the "Shema," found in Deuteronomy 6:5.

6. John Wesley said that our neighbor is "not only thy friend, thy kinsman, or thy acquaintance: not only the virtuous, the friendly, him that loves thee, that prevents or returns thy kindness; but every child of man, every human creature, every soul which God hath made; . . . not excepting him whom thou knowest to be evil or unthankful, him that still despitefully uses and persecutes thee; him though shalt love *as thyself;* with the same invariable thirst after his happiness in every kind; the same unwearied care to screen him from whatever might grieve or hurt either his soul or body." John Wesley, *Sermons on Several Occasions,* vol. 1 (London: Wesleyan Conference Office, 1864), 73. Maybe read that a few times to really understand it, but wow, huh?

12 | Tony

1. Now, before you get all hot and bothered, this book isn't about your viewpoint or mine on a specific hot-button topic. Try to set aside your stance on this and just see Tony. As I wrote this chapter, I felt the need to explain my own views further, but Jesus didn't feel that way. He didn't feel the need to constantly explain himself and his intentions. Instead, he just hung out with people without worrying about how it might be interpreted and met them where they were. I'm trying to be more like that. A lot of churches talk a good game about loving people like Tony, but when it comes down to it, they have no place for them. I don't have all the answers, but I do know that at Embrace we do our best to live out the promise of Jesus with the warmth that our name suggests. This sometimes takes us into what feels like uncharted territory in the church world. But it's not uncharted for

Jesus! We have decided that our call is to love radically, to share God's grace and truth, and to do life with anyone who is being drawn to God.

2. All-nighters were always a bad choice for me. I'd get to whatever test I had the next day exhausted and buzzing from the six pots of coffee I had drunk to stay awake.

3. This story about the leper and Jesus is from Matthew 8:1–4, which I've paraphrased.

4. Many studies show that touch impacts our emotional wellness almost more than anything else. Some smart neuroscientist named David Linden observed that of our five senses as humans, touch is the most important and yet often the most overlooked. David J. Linden, "The Science of Touching and Feeling," January 19, 2017, *TED Radio Hour*, TEDx Talk video, 14:15, www.npr.org/2017/01/20/510627341/why-is-it-important-to-be-touched.

5. Bec and I first touched hands at Campus Park in Sioux Falls. It was the first time that she came to visit me from Grand Forks, North Dakota, where she went to college. Campus Park was just a block from my house. We walked over, sat on the swings, and after an hour or so, I finally gained the courage to reach out and grab her hand. Inside of me there were fireworks. I think I even remember seeing angels dancing in the sky. Okay, maybe not angels, but you get the picture.

6. Gordie, you are one of my favorites. Love you. Billy II.

7. This makes me think of Elliott and ET. #ETphonehome

8. There's power in touch. It's why when we're touched inappropriately or by someone we don't want to be touched by, even if it doesn't hurt us physically, it impacts our soul. If this is a part of your story, I'm so sorry. I can't encourage you enough to talk with someone, to tell someone.

9. The friend who said this to me was Chad Pickard. If you ever need some wisdom, go find him. He typically starts his morning at the downtown Coffea Roasterie in Sioux Falls. Then you can find him at Spoke-N-Sport. He's like Yoda "but better looking." His words, not mine!

10. John Wesley had a good word on this: "Though we cannot think alike, may we not love alike?" John Wesley, *The Works of the*

Reverend John Wesley, vol. 1 (New York: Emory and Waugh, 1831), 347.

13 | Mark

1. If our spiritual intensity doesn't lead us to have more kindness, gentleness, self-control, and love in our lives, we're not becoming more holy—we're moving further away from God.
2. This is typically what happens. A church isn't "deep" enough, so the person goes looking for a church that is. They're satisfied for a few months, but once again the new church isn't deep enough, so they uproot and go to another church. Free wisdom: if you are constantly jumping from one church to the next, one relationship to the next, one job to the next, one (fill in the blank) to the next, the problem is you! You might try to excuse it by saying "the Holy Spirit is leading me," but the God I know talks a lot about being faithful and consistent and not sporadically jumping from place to place.
3. I've always wondered which church is considered the receding hairline? The gallbladder? Body hair? I'll stop!
4. See Matthew 23:25, 33.
5. Scott Sauls is the pastor at Christ Presbyterian Church in Nashville, Tennessee. He's one of the best people to follow on Twitter (@ScottSauls). There are few pastors I respect more than Scott for their godly wisdom or the life they live! Scott Sauls (@ScottSauls), "The 'Grace Pharisee' is judgmental toward judgmental people," Twitter, February 28, 2020, twitter.com /scottsauls/status/1233406953591889920.
6. My good friend Roger Fredrikson would always say, "Adam, I'm just a recovering sinner in need of Jesus." I miss you dearly, Roger.
7. This story about Nicodemus and Jesus is from John 3:1–21, which I've paraphrased.
8. I'm a Christian, so I'm not into smoking things through a diffuser. #essentialoils #justkidding
9. Thank goodness for field notes! There are so many nuances when it comes to loving people. Yes, we should never start by shutting people out of our lives. But there are certain people who, after we get to know them, we realize are toxic and need to

walk away from. From toxic boyfriends and high-maintenance clients to abusive family members, there are people we will never please no matter how hard we try. Instead we can love them from a distance. Read this a few times if you need to. Translation: Don't let the Marks in your life dictate how you live. Jesus is Lord. The Marks of the world aren't.

10. I will say this: if reading our Bibles and "going deeper" doesn't lead us to forgiving others, befriending sinners, giving money away, loving Jesus, serving when no one's looking, and developing a heart for the lost, we're not becoming disciples. Instead we're becoming Pharisees who are further from Jesus, not closer. I love my Bible. I would encourage anyone to dive into the Word. I just don't want to ever see myself becoming a Pharisee or pastor of a church of Pharisees. I want to call out the inconsistencies I see between the "religious" and people who follow Jesus with action and not just words. I also want to be careful to call these things out in love—not in hate, not in an accusatory way.

14 | Captain

1. This story about Legion and Jesus is from Mark 5:1–20, which I've paraphrased.

2. I picture him looking like a combination of Bigfoot and that kid from *Teen Wolf*!

3. I don't think I need to say this, but I will in case you need to hear it: you are not Jesus. Yes, you should be like Jesus and love like Jesus, but it's not your job to save or fix people. What I'm saying is that if a person is really unhealthy, you need to point him to professional help. And if it's an abusive situation, don't get closer—run! Run as far and as fast as you can.

4. How do you distinguish between the two? Pray and ask for God's direction. Put yourself in the other person's shoes. What would you need in that situation? If there's a trusted mutual friend, ask that friend for advice.

5. It's healthy to acknowledge when we're hurt by someone. Brushing things under the rug isn't Jesus-like even though we often think it is. "Just move on and you'll be fine." Yes, we should be

quick to forgive and not easily offended, but when we're truly hurt by another person, it's healthy to say it. It might be the start of healing for the other person as well.

6. I've known since I was eight years old that I wanted to adopt a child when I got married. Have you considered adoption? How wonderful would it be if every child in the world had a forever home. You can't change the world, but you can change the world for one child.

7. I love you, Becca. I'm so proud of the person you are. Thanks for letting me share a part of your story.

8. Sometimes you're going to screw up. You're going to try and love someone and unknowingly cause more harm than good. It's going to happen! One night when I was in elementary school, my dad saw four guys who were trying to get their car started in a parking lot across the street from our house. It was late and dark. Because my dad is nice and basically MacGyver, he walked across the street and offered to help. Within minutes, he had their car started. The men all thanked my dad and drove off. A good deed done by my dad, right? Well, not exactly. The next day my parents read in the newspaper that four men had broken into the business across the street from our house the night before and driven away with hundreds of dollars—the four men my dad helped! Years later, we're still talking about how my dad "helped start their getaway car"! (P.S. If you don't know who MacGyver is, you've never lived.)

15 | Shirley

1. Just to rant for a minute: Why are those bins so small?! I get so annoyed at the guy who takes five minutes to shove his luggage in when everyone else is waiting in line behind him. It's always complete chaos. Tip for airlines everywhere: *make the bins bigger.* Okay, end of rant.

2. On flights over states such as South Dakota, Nebraska, and Colorado, I always love hearing what to do in case the plane lands in water. We have a better chance of winning the Powerball lottery than our plane landing in water, but let's hear it.

3. Have you ever noticed that planes are the only place in the world

that still use old-school telephones? Like the kind with a cord and everything? When will they all just switch to a regular microphone? Remember the phones they had at A&W Restaurants?

4. This story about the woman and Jesus is from Luke 8:42–48, which I've paraphrased.

5. A throng, not a thong. That would definitely be a different type of greeting.

6. I can't count the number of cups of coffee I drank as I wrote this book!

16 | Running Man

1. This story about Jesus and the man whose ear was cut off is from Luke 22:47–51, which I've paraphrased.

2. Think Mike Tyson biting Evander Holyfield's ear off—that's pretty much what this was like.

3. I wish we had a video of the man's ear growing back! It'd go viral within minutes! A total miracle.

4. The past few months, I've been pretty proud of myself. I hadn't been given the finger while driving for three months straight! But then my streak broke yesterday. Buddy, I promise I didn't try to cut you off!

17 | Bill

1. Something I've realized lately is that people who are quick to speak, give advice, or label themselves an expert on (fill in the blank) rarely ever have much experience with (fill in the blank). People who have great wisdom, endless experience, and actually are experts at (fill in the blank) are slow to speak, slow to give advice, and humbly quiet about (fill in the blank). Examples are marriage, parenting, leadership, business, following Jesus, sports, life—everything. Pro tip: be *very* slow to give advice on things that you have little to no experience with.

2. Every month, the light bulbs outside our garage would disappear. I thought, *Maybe someone really needs light bulbs?* I found out later that light bulbs are used to make meth. The more you know.

3. Pro tip: if you're ever passing through Minnesota, do not miss Minnesota's Largest Candy Store on Highway 169! It's a much

bigger deal than the Mall of America. You can thank me later. This one tip might be worth the price of this book.

4. If I ever offer you food, do not eat or accept it. But there is one exception: my chocolate chip cookies. I use my Grandma Dahle's recipe, and they are *amazing*!

5. In case you forgot, you're a pretty messy person too. I pray you and I will never forget our mess.

6. These were all actual Facebook comments on a recent news story about a sex offender.

7. Each time Bill asked about borrowing my lawn mower, I didn't want to let him borrow it. Secretly, I thought he should buy his own mower and gas. I would like to think I'm a generous person, but I found out that generosity goes away when it comes to my lawn mower! Sad, right? Looking back, I thank God that Bill would confidently ask for my lawn mower. It was good for my soul. And really, was it ever my lawn mower to begin with?

8. Yep, in your home! Gasp!

9. Note to Christians who want to go really "deep": depth isn't found by reading the Bible more; it's found in moments like this after reading your Bible more.

10. Working on this house has been our version of *Fixer Upper*! I've always dreamed of being Chip.

11. Good theology is so important. I truly believe that, now more than ever. My hope, though, is that you don't stop with just "loving Jesus and having good theology." Instead, love Jesus, have good theology, and let that transform you, which will no doubt result in radically loving people like Jesus did.

18 | Russ and F—Man

1. The fighter was Michael Chandler, a three-time MMA world champion.

2. Thanks for the tickets, Jones!

3. This was Tyler, my realtor friend, who I wrote about earlier.

4. Today we know this celebration as Palm Sunday—one of my favorite holidays. Each Palm Sunday, we have donkeys at the church I pastor. Kids can pet and get their pictures taken with the donkeys. I think I enjoy the donkeys more than the kids do.

5. This story about the two blind men and Jesus is from Matthew 20:28–34, which I've paraphrased.

6. Matthew 20:33.

7. These types of guys should be the VIPs in our churches, the people we base daily decisions around. Not the big givers. Not the loudest complainers. Not the people who have been part of the church for the longest time. Instead, the VIPs in Jesus's eyes are people like the two guys at the fight and the two blind men on the side of the road.

8. Trust me, this would actually be the go-to response of a lot of Christians!

19 | A. C. Kidd

1. This nickname reminds me of A. C. Slater. I dream of looking like A. C. Slater! Tight curls. Biceps bigger than my head. Dimples. Dude. I mean, Preppy!

2. A. C. Kidd stands for Angry College Kid, just so you know.

3. If you haven't read it before, I would encourage you to pause and read all of Luke 15 before continuing.

4. I've been a die-hard Bengals fan since I was three years old. I remember Super Bowl XXIII (January 1989) like it was yesterday, and sometimes I still cry thinking about John Taylor scoring the winning touchdown for the 49ers. I also really don't like the Steelers. I kid you not, you can tell me your political views, that you've committed a crime, or that you've even thought about slashing my tires, and I'll still love you. But if you tell me you're a Steelers fan? I'll start questioning your integrity and whether or not you have a soul.

5. Sad fact about Sioux Falls, South Dakota: For centuries we have lived without a Chipotle or Chick-fil-A. But God has heard our prayers!

6. At the end of Jesus's conversations with people, once he's clearly established a relationship, once they clearly know that he loves them unconditionally, then Jesus tells them to "go and sin no more"! If you are eager and *excited* to share the "go and sin no more" piece with a person, you shouldn't speak. God will use someone else because your heart is in the wrong place. Before

telling others to stop sinning, you might need to start by grasping the depth of your own sin.

20 | Ted, Ambrose Lekol, Jillian, and Jerry

1. Don't live in Sioux Falls, but want to talk? Come find me on social.

2. If you end up trying this or something similar, I'd love to hear about it.

3. This was something I felt led to do and had planned to do a year ago, but each time I chickened out. What kind of crazy person would sit at a desk outside and invite people to talk to him? Well, today I couldn't find any excuse not to do it, so here I am.

4. It's been years, and I'm still trying to figure out who let the dogs out.

5. I've learned that I need to quickly tell at least one person what I'm feeling challenged to do—otherwise I'll convince myself not to do it.

6. This gives us Westerners some perspective, doesn't it? My kids don't even walk a block to school. I drop them off each day right outside the door of their school.

7. We partner with an organization called Mission-Haiti. They are the real heroes. You can find out more and sponsor a child at www.mission-haiti.org. I think you should sponsor a child. If you decide to do so, let me know!

8. Thanks again, Grant, for your help.

9. If you're ever in Sioux Falls, come find the #SiouxFallsWings and get a picture taken with them!

10. You can check out some of Jillian's other work on Instagram at @JillianArtistry.

11. I've since made my makeshift sidewalk office a fairly regular thing. I've prayed with people. Grieved with a young mom as she found out her dad had terminal cancer. Listened to people's stories. Been present with many as they've cried. One guy had a guitar and ended up singing to me. I've sat in complete silence with a person who I think just wanted to be near someone. One person who walked past me the other day said it best: "Everyone needs someone to listen."

21 | *You*

1. When someone tells me that I preached a great message, my go-to response is, "In the Old Testament, God spoke through a donkey. Maybe he can do it again?" I struggle with compliments.

2. We seriously need more people named Zebedee in this world. What a great name!

3. John 20:2.

4. Fun fact: John was the only one of the twelve disciples to die of natural causes. God surely loved him. Lucky dog!

5. Henri Nouwen (@HenriNouwen), "Five lies of identity," Twitter, November 23, 2018, https://twitter.com/henrinouwen/status /1066006327862935553?lang=en. You can read more of Nouwen's heart around this in his book with Philip Roderick, *Beloved: Henri Nouwen in Conversation* (London: Canterbury Press, 2007).

6. John is given credit for writing the gospel of John, along with the letters 1, 2, and 3 John.

7. 1 John 3:16, paraphrased. I couldn't leave this out! It's a complete tangent but so good. So, John tells us all about what real love is, and then he says, "We love because he first loved us" (1 John 4:19, NIV).

   We love others *why*?

   Because he first loved us.

   We've been so loved with an extravagant, unconditional love (even in the moments when we don't deserve it), and as a result we can't help but extend the same extravagant, unconditional love to others (even in the moments they don't deserve it). We not only want to share that love, but we have to! When God has loved us so well, how could we possibly keep it to ourselves?

   We love others *how*?

   Same answer: because he first loved us.

   It is only with God's love inside of us that we are able to love others. On our own, we have very little love. I've read through the words of John more times than I can count, but a few weeks back, something hit me for the very first time. I'll just let John say it: "Dear friends, since God loved us so much, we surely ought to love each other. No one has ever seen God. But if we love each other, God lives in us, and his love is made perfect in us" (1 John 4:11–12, paraphrased).

God loves us so much—we surely should love each other. No one has ever seen God (yep, I agree), but if we love others, his love is seen in us. Not our broken, self-centered love, but his perfect, unending, unconditional love is seen by others in us. In our words and actions. In our attitude and lives. What? Amazing! Truly wonderful.

But here's the part that stuck out to me: when we love others, his love is made perfect and complete, not only to the people we are loving but *to us* as well. In the moment of loving others, we experience God's perfect love ourselves. Within us. Inside us.

Why? Because in the moment of loving others, we are most like Jesus.

Our words are most like his.

Our attitude and thoughts are most like his.

Our actions are most like his.

Our love is most like his.

And the best part: our *hearts* are most like his.

His love is made perfect inside us and for us.

I've often wondered why it feels so good to love others. When you love with no strings attached. When you love expecting nothing in return. When you love extravagantly with everything you have. When you see the best version of people, not the worst. When you love like a little kid does. This is why! His love is made perfect inside of us.

When we truly love others, even with our brokenness and imperfections, we are made complete. We are made whole. The cracks are filled in with the perfect love of Jesus. The same love that John knew firsthand.

8. See John 3:16.

9. I share the full story of growing up in church in my book *Talking with God* (Colorado Springs, CO: WaterBrook, 2017).

10. If I ever would have been legitimately sick on a Sunday morning, I would have died. My parents would have never believed me.

11. Years later, and I still remember almost all of the prayers.

12. 1 John 3:1, NIV.

13. A few Sundays ago, I was incredibly discouraged. I was questioning the message I was about to preach. Feeling completely inadequate to be used by God and even deeper, I was questioning my worth. Until I had an older man in the church walk up to me. He's a dear brother, and he could tell something was off in me without me saying a word. He put his hand on my shoulder, looked me in the eyes, and said, "Adam, you are so loved by God." Tears flooded my eyes. What a wonderful thing to be fully and completely loved by God. Love you, Gene McDaniel.

14. A devotional I can't recommend more highly is *Emotionally Healthy Spirituality Day by Day* by Peter Scazzero (Grand Rapids, MI: Zondervan, 2008). It has been life changing for me.

About Adam.

ADAM WEBER is the founder and lead pastor of Embrace, a multisite church based in Sioux Falls, South Dakota. The author of *Talking with God,* he also hosts a podcast called *The Conversation.* Adam still cheers for the Cincinnati Bengals but no longer drives a Rambler. He's married to his wife, Becky, and has four kids: Hudson, Wilson, Grayson, and Anderson. He also has seven chickens, two dogs, and three fish, but what he really wants is a sheep.

You can find out more at adamweber.com.

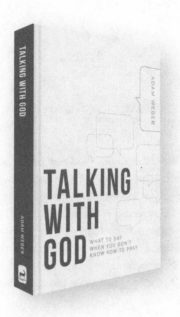

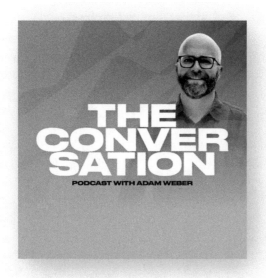

THE
CONVERSATION
PODCAST

NEW CONVERSATIONS RELEASED WEEKLY

WATERBROOK